£4·50

The Plains Indians

Rosemary Rees and Sue Styles

LONGMAN

Longman Group UK Limited
Longman House, Burnt Mill, Harlow, Essex,
CM20 2JE, England and Associated Companies

First published 1993
Second impression 1993

ISBN 0 582 08251 X

Set in 11/15pt Bodoni (Lasercomp)
Produced by Longman Singapore Publishers Pte Ltd
Printed in Singapore

The publishers policy is to use paper
manufactured from sustainable forests.

Designed by Michael Harris

Illustrations:
Pages 5, 6, 7, 9, 13, 16, 26, 36, 44, 47, 49, 60,
64, 69 Tony Richardson
Pages 8, 20, 24, 31, 46 Peter Dennis
Page 10 Kathy Baxendale

Cover photograph:
Peter Newark's Western Americana

We are grateful to the following for
permission to reproduce photographs:

American Heritage Center, University of
Wyoming, page 21 below; American
Museum of Natural History, Department of
Library Services, page 6 bottom (neg. no.
310670), 6 top (neg. no. 317281); Bridgeman
Art Library, pages 7 left, 25 left, 52, 71;
British Library (Newspaper Library) pages
55; British Museum (Museum of Mankind)
page 40 centre; taken from *Catlin's North
American Indian Portfolio*, 1844, pages 20,
27, 32; taken from *The Century*, Nov. 1890,
page 45; Colorado Historical Society, page
62; Corcoran Gallery of Art, Gift of William
Wilson Corcoran, page 30; Denver Art
Museum, page 26; Mary Evans Picture
Library, page 44; Werner Forman Archive,
pages 21 above, 33 above and below, 40 left
and right; Thomas Gilcrease Institute of
American History and Art, Tulsa,
Oklahoma, pages 14, 41, 67 above; taken
from *Harper's Monthly*, pages 31 (May
1891), 38 (July 1891); Mansell Collection,
pages 24, 50; Metropolitan Museum of Art,
New York, page 11; Missouri Historical
Society (neg. no. Wo-Haw 326) page 78
above; Museum für Völkerkunde, Berlin (©
Bildarchiv Preussischer Kulturbesitz 1993)
page 6 centre; National Archives Canada,
Ottawa (neg. no. C–114494) page 15; Peter
Newark's Western Americana, pages 25
right, 37, 51, 54, 57, 63, 67 below, 69;
Oklahoma Historical Society Museum,
Oklahoma City, page 23; Roger-Viollet, page
12; Salamander Books (artwork by Lois
Sloan from *The Native Americans*, 1991)
page 7 right; Smithsonian Institution, pages
35 above (neg. no. 1668), 35 below (neg. no.
75–4628), 68 (neg. no. 3195–A), 75 (neg. no.
55–752), 76 above (neg. no. 55–018), 76
below (neg. no. 76–4941), 78 below (neg. no.
83–7738); Southwest Museum, Los Angeles
(photo no. CT.1) page 72; Frank Spooner
Pictures, page 80; University of Oklahoma,
Western History Collections, page 77.

We are grateful to Random House UK Ltd
and Hilda Neihardt Petri as Trustee of the
Neihardt Trust for extracts from *Black Elk
Speaks* by J. Neihardt.

Contents

J. Grasset S.ᵗ Sauveur inv. direx   J. Laroque Sculp.

Sauvage Iroquois

1 The first Americans

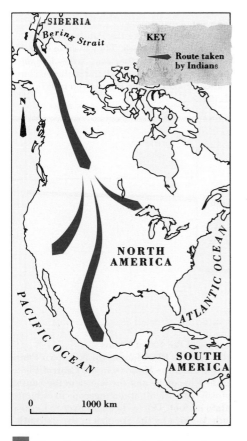

Twenty thousand years ago America was not a separate continent as it is today. Look at the map on this page. You can see that North America was linked to Asia across what is now known as the Bering Strait. Great herds of animals used to wander from Asia across this huge land bridge. People followed them. Why did they do this? Geologists and archaeologists have dug through the frozen rocks of Alaska and the hot, sandy deserts of Arizona and discovered ancient stone fireplaces and arrow-heads made many thousands of years ago. These Stone Age people were wandering nomads, hunter-gatherers who followed the vast herds of animals wherever they went. They moved slowly down through North America, following the animal trails. In the end the trails led some of these people to the very heart of North America – the Great Plains. Others, like the Aztecs, went south to settle in what is now Mexico. Others carried on further down into South America, like the Incas who settled in Peru.

About nine thousand years ago this movement of people and animals came to an end. The sea came crashing across the great land bridge. America was cut off from Asia for ever. By this time, the people whom Europeans later called 'Indians' were firmly settled in North, Central and South America.

1 How the Indians came to America. Historians think these were the routes taken by the people who crossed from Asia to America during the Stone Age.

1 How do you think historians have been able to trace the routes taken by these people so many thousands of years ago?

The North American Indians

By the fifteenth century there were many different Indian tribes living in North America. They lived on the dry plains, in the rocky mountains, the wooded valleys and the icy wastes inside the Arctic Circle. They had very different ways of life. Some went on living in a hand-to-mouth way, surviving on food which they could hunt and gather. Others found ways of irrigating and farming the land. Those who settled in the fertile east farmed and fished. Some Indians developed wonderful skills of stalking, tool-making and archery. These different ways of life did not change for thousands of years. The first big change came during the fifteenth and sixteenth centuries, when people from Europe began to cross the Atlantic Ocean and settle in America. Three hundred years after this, their descendants began to move west, across the Great Plains. Here the Plains Indians had lived and hunted for centuries. We shall later look in detail at the lives of the Plains Indians and how the Europeans changed their way of life.

Fisher-folk of the north-west coast
In this narrow strip of land, with the Pacific to the west and huge mountains to the east, Indians like the Nootka and, the Haida fished for salmon in the deep fast-flowing rivers. They lived in villages of wooden houses and carved tall totem poles.

3 Nez Perce woman.

Gatherers of the west
In this dry, desolate area tribes like the Paiute and the Shoshoni gathered seeds and berries. They lived in little huts made of sticks and twigs. Further east, tribes like the Flathead and the Nez Perce also hunted and gathered, but they fished for salmon too. The Nez Perce lived in skin tipis like the Plains Indians.

2 The different parts of North America and the ways of life of the different Indians who lived there.

4 Navaho Indian.

Farmers and hunters of the south-western deserts, mountains and grasslands
Tribes like the Apache, the Navaho and the Mohave Indians hunted deer and rabbit. They grew corn, beans and marrows. They wove cotton cloth with wonderful patterns, and made pottery and baskets. Apaches lived in small huts made of twigs and branches. The Navaho lived in small log huts, sometimes daubed with clay.

1 There were, as you have seen, many different Indian tribes in North America. Look at the map on pages 6 and 7.
a) How were their ways of life different?
b) Did these different Indians have anything in common with each other?

5 Sioux Indian woman.

Hunters of the Great Plains
Tribes like the Blackfoot in the Northern Plains, the Sioux and the Mandan in the Central Plains and the Comanche and the Kiowa in the Southern Plains lived difficult and dangerous lives hunting buffalo on foot. Horses brought over to Central and South America by the Spanish in the sixteenth century drifted north. By the end of the eighteenth century, the Plains Indians had horses, and their lives improved. They hunted on horseback. They lived in buffalo-skin tipis.

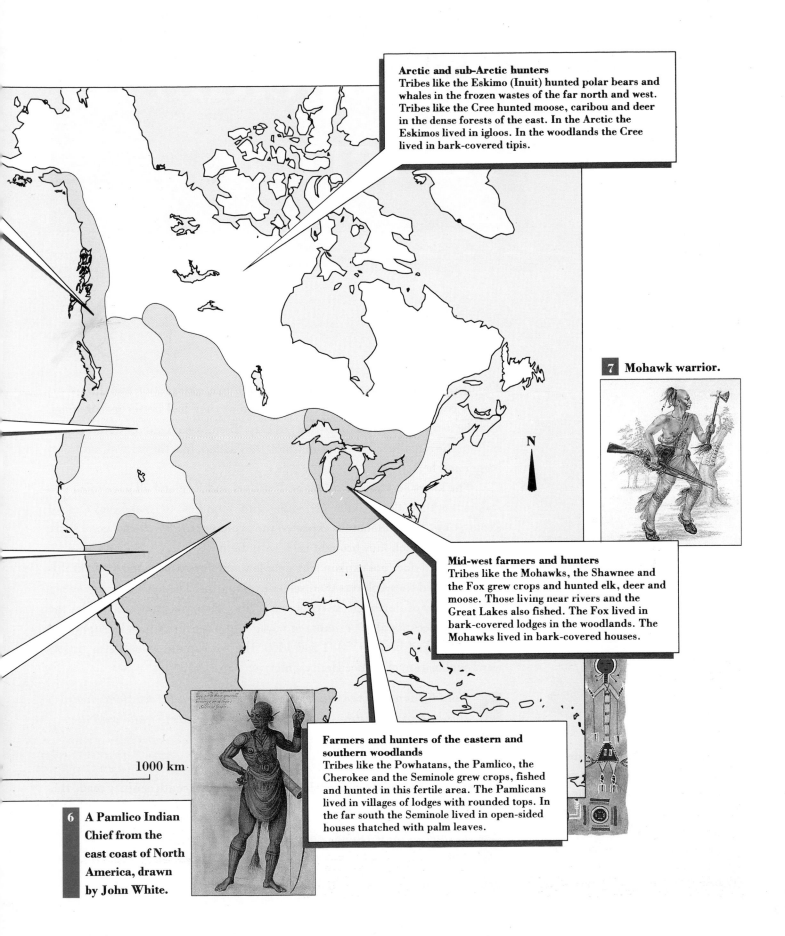

Arctic and sub-Arctic hunters
Tribes like the Eskimo (Inuit) hunted polar bears and whales in the frozen wastes of the far north and west. Tribes like the Cree hunted moose, caribou and deer in the dense forests of the east. In the Arctic the Eskimos lived in igloos. In the woodlands the Cree lived in bark-covered tipis.

7 Mohawk warrior.

N

Mid-west farmers and hunters
Tribes like the Mohawks, the Shawnee and the Fox grew crops and hunted elk, deer and moose. Those living near rivers and the Great Lakes also fished. The Fox lived in bark-covered lodges in the woodlands. The Mohawks lived in bark-covered houses.

1000 km

Farmers and hunters of the eastern and southern woodlands
Tribes like the Powhatans, the Pamlico, the Cherokee and the Seminole grew crops, fished and hunted in this fertile area. The Pamlicans lived in villages of lodges with rounded tops. In the far south the Seminole lived in open-sided houses thatched with palm leaves.

6 A Pamlico Indian Chief from the east coast of North America, drawn by John White.

2 Europeans in America

The fifteenth and sixteenth centuries were a time of exploration and discovery. Sailors could now make these voyages because they had better instruments, like the astrolabe and the quadrant, to help them to navigate in waters out of sight of the coastline. The ships in which they sailed, like the caravel, were also bigger and better.

The kings and queens of Spain, Portugal and England all gave money to sailors so that they could get ships and supplies to make voyages of exploration. These monarchs expected the explorers to give them a good share of the riches which they brought back with them.

This still does not explain *why* people wanted to explore the world at this time. How did the explorers themselves explain this? Diego Gomes was one of Prince Henry of Portugal's sea captains. Prince Henry is known as 'Henry the Navigator' because of the number of voyages of discovery which he supported and encouraged between 1434 and 1460. His sea captain gives a straightforward explanation of Prince Henry's motive:

 Gold is found in great quantities. When my Lord Prince Henry heard this he sent expeditions to these countries overseas to trade with them.

Diego Gomes, diary entry, fifteenth century

A sailor who went to the Spice Islands in the early sixteenth century made this report:

3 *In three of these islands grows abundance of nutmeg. After these islands there are five others, where all the cloves grow.*

Anonymous, *Book of Duarte Barbosa*, 1524

1 Using an astrolabe. The astrolabe was best worked by two men. One held the astrolabe up by the ring at the top and moved the pointer until it pointed at the Pole Star. The other man read the angle on the dial. This gave the latitude – that is how far north or south they were.

Vasco da Gama gave two main reasons for coming to India during his first voyage from Portugal, 1497–9:

> **4** *Four boats approached us from the land, and asked us of what nation we were. On the following day the captain-major sent men ashore. People asked what he was seeking so far away from home. He told them that we came in search of Christians and spices.*
>
> Quoted by E. G. Ravenstein, *First Voyage of Vasco de Gama, 1497–1499*, 1898

As you can see on the map, the old trade routes to the East were overland. Traders brought back precious goods such as spices, silks and perfumes. These routes passed through lands called the Ottoman Empire. People in these lands became angry and started to demand high taxes when Europeans crossed their lands. One way of avoiding this would be to sail directly to the East. No one, as yet, had found a direct sea-route to India and the Indies.

5 Old trade routes.

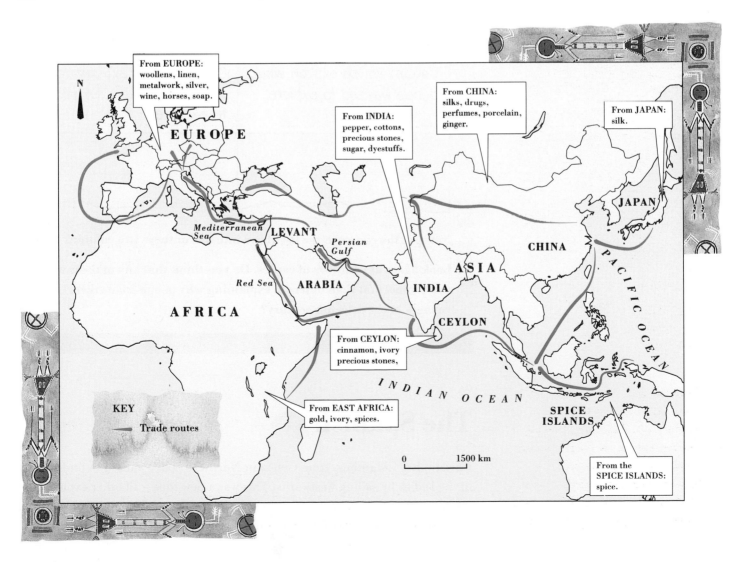

From EUROPE: woollens, linen, metalwork, silver, wine, horses, soap.

From INDIA: pepper, cottons, precious stones, sugar, dyestuffs.

From CHINA: silks, drugs, perfumes, porcelain, ginger.

From JAPAN: silk.

From CEYLON: cinnamon, ivory precious stones,

From EAST AFRICA: gold, ivory, spices.

From the SPICE ISLANDS: spice.

KEY
— Trade routes

0   1500 km

As you have seen, European people began to explore unknown areas of the world during the fifteenth century. You may have found a number of causes for this, like those in the list below.

a) Kings and queens gave money to sailors to help them to get ships and supplies for the journey.

b) People wanted to have spices like nutmeg and cloves. These could only be found in the Spice Islands.

c) There were now better instruments for navigation, like the quadrant and the astrolabe.

d) There were now better ships, like the caravel, which made long journeys by sea possible.

e) It was becoming more difficult for Western Europeans to travel overland to the east to bring back goods such as spices.

f) Some explorers, like Vasco da Gama, wanted to meet people who were not Christians in other lands and to persuade them to become Christians.

1 Draw a table with headings like this one:

Causes which explain why people wanted to explore.	Causes which explain what made it possible for people to explore.

    Now put the causes in the list above into one of these two columns

2 Look again at your lists of causes. Do you think that any of these were more important than others in explaining why people made these voyages in the fifteenth century?

The Spanish

Christopher Columbus, from Genoa in Northern Italy, wanted to find a route to the Indies by sailing westwards. This was a new idea – all other explorers so far had been sailing south and west, exploring Africa. Columbus could not find anyone in Italy to support his plans for a voyage so he went to Queen Isabella of

Castile, in Spain. She was more than pleased to support him. She would gain great glory (and wealth) for her country if he discovered a new route to the Indies, and brought back gold, silver, spices and silks. So the day of Columbus's departure finally dawned.

> **6** *Half an hour before sunrise, I set my course for the Canary Islands, which are in the Ocean Sea* [Atlantic Ocean], *from there to set off on a voyage that will last until I arrive in the Indies.*

Christopher Columbus, journal entry, 2 August 1492

7 Christopher Columbus, painted in 1519, 13 years after his death.

On 12 October 1492, Christopher Columbus (or Cristobal Colon, as his Spanish sailors called him) anchored off a beach on a tropical island. He believed that he had reached the Indies. He and his men named the place San Salvador, which means 'Holy Saviour'. He called the people whom he met 'Indians'. He then went off to look for the Emperor of China. Columbus was wrong. He had not discovered a new route to the Indies and he had not landed in China. He had, instead, landed on one of the islands which form part of what we now call the West Indies. He did not know that the huge land mass of North and South America lay between Europe and China.

Columbus died in 1506, still believing that he had found a new route to the Indies. He was probably not the first European to set foot in North America. There is strong evidence to suggest that the Vikings landed there in about 1000AD. There is even evidence that some sailors from Bristol, England, landed in North America in 1481. Columbus's voyages were, however, important. Afterwards, many people sailed over to North America to trade and to settle there.

Indians and the Spanish

Those parts of America which the Spaniards took as their own were hot, sticky and mosquito-plagued islands. The Spanish soldiers hated having to spend time there.

It was only after Hernan Cortes, a Spanish soldier, landed with an army in 1519 in what is now Mexico that the Spanish began to be pleased that they had lands in this 'new world'. High on a plateau in central Mexico stood the huge, rich and splendid city of Tenochtitlan. This is how it seemed to one of the men who travelled with Cortes:

> **8** *We admired the high towers, pyramids and other buildings, all of stone, which rose from the water. It was all so wonderful that I do not know how to describe this first glimpse of things never heard of, seen or dreamed of before.*

Bernal Diaz , journal entry, about 1520

9 Cortes and his conquistadors, from an Aztec manuscript.

guzmā.   mchvacā.

Tenochtitlan was the capital city of the Aztecs and their Emperor Montezuma II. Greedy for the gold, silver and precious stones which they found there, Cortes and his men eventually destroyed the city in 1521 and claimed that part of America for Spain.

Fired with enthusiasm at this new Spanish conquest, hundreds of Spaniards sailed for America in search of land and riches. They were prepared to kill the American Indians to get hold of these. Many Indians died, either at the hands of the 'conquistadors' (conquerors) or from the diseases which the Europeans brought with them. Thousands died from measles, whooping-cough, chicken-pox and influenza. All of these were unknown in America before the coming of the Spanish.

Later, Spanish men and women settled in South and Central America. They set up cattle ranches, vineyards and tea plantations. They built fine houses. They depended, however, on the labour of Indian slaves. Without them the Spaniards could not become rich and successful in their new lands in America.

Look at this drawing carefully.
1 Which one do you think is Cortes?
2 How would you describe the difference between the conquistadors and the Indians in this drawing?

3 Put together a list of all the
   different causes and results of the
   coming of the Spanish to America,
   and then complete this chart.
4 Were any of these causes and effects
   more important than others?
   If you think so, try to explain why.

CAUSES

EFFECTS

THE
SPANISH
IN
AMERICA

The English

In 1497 an Italian sailor, John Cabot, landed on an island off the coast of North America. He named it Newfoundland and claimed it for England. Cabot had found no support in Italy but King Henry VII of England agreed to give him money for his voyage. He told Cabot that he should 'sail to all parts, regions and wastes of the eastern, western and northern seas'. This was the beginning of English exploration of North America. It was not until the reign of Henry VII's granddaughter, Elizabeth I, that England began to challenge Spain's position in America. Though Spanish monarchs claimed the whole of North America, they did not hold any lands north of what is now Florida. This meant that the English (and later the French) were able to explore and claim lands in North America for themselves without challenge from Spain.

During the reigns of Elizabeth I and her successor and cousin, James I, English people began to settle in lands on the eastern coast of North America. The map on page 16 shows you who settled where, and when. By 1732 the English had taken over all the lands on the eastern seaboard of North America. These lands formed the thirteen English colonies of North America.

Setting up these colonies was not always easy. In 1607 Captain Christopher Newport landed with three ships in Chesapeake bay, Virginia. He founded Jamestown, named after King James I of England. Unfortunately, the settlement was near a marshy swamp which swarmed with malaria-carrying mosquitoes. Many of the settlers died from malaria; others caught and died from dysentery. Local tribes of Indians attacked them. The Indians resented the English settlers who had taken their lands. One of the settlers wrote:

> **10** *There were never Englishmen left in a foreign country in such misery as we were in this newly-discovered Virginia.*
>
> George Percy, letter, 1607

5 Make a list of the different
   reasons which you can find for
   English people settling in
   North America.
   a) Do any of these reasons
   occur more than others?
   Look back at the work which
   you did on the reasons for the
   Spanish coming to America.
   b) Which reasons for the
   English coming to America are
   similar to ones for Spanish
   exploration of America?
   c) Which reasons for the
   English coming to America are
   different from the ones for
   Spanish exploration of
   America?
   d) 'The English and the
   Spanish had the same reasons
   for wanting to explore and
   settle in America?'
   Do you agree with this?
   Explain why, or why not.

11 Penn's treaty with the Indians. Painted by Edward Hicks, an Englishman, in the 1840s, this scene shows Sir William Penn making a treaty with the Indians who lived in the area which he wanted to colonise in 1681.

Indians and the English

Some time before the founding of Jamestown, five tribes from the Iroquois-speaking group of Indians, banded into a group led by the most powerful of their chiefs. Powhatan. This was then known as the 'Powhatan Confederacy'. There was peace between the Indians and the English settlers for some time. An Englishman, John Rolfe, married Pocohontas, Powhatan's daughter. Sadly, she died during a visit to England. When Powhatan himself died, his brother, Opechancanough, became chief of the Confederacy. He feared that the English settlers would, in the end, overwhelm the Indians. In 1622 he attacked Jamestown and killed over 300 people – about one third of the population. The settlers fought back and pushed the Indian tribes inland.

Some English settlers, however, built up good relationships with the Indians. For example, the governor of Virginia in 1676, Sir William Berkeley, exchanged goods made in England with the Indians in return for furs and deerskins.

William Penn founded the town of Pennsylvania. He was honest in his dealings with the Indians. In 1682 he said to the Indians: 'I desire to enjoy it with your consent, that we may always live together as neighbours and friends.' In 1686 they promised him as much land as a man could walk in three days. Penn took only what he walked, slowly, in a day and a half.

It is difficult to know what the Indians thought about the English settlers. They did not use a written form of language or communication, and so we have no descriptions of their feelings. We do have, though, what one of the first settlers in Virginia wrote down from what Powhatan said do him.

Think you I am not so simple, not to know it is better to eat good meat, lie well and sleep quietly with my women and children, being your friend, than be forced to fly from all, to lie cold in the woods, and be so hunted by you that I can neither rest, eat nor sleep.

Powhatan, Iroquois chief, to John Smith, 1608

Indians must have been astonished when they first saw white people with their strange way of dressing and their strange speech. They must have wondered at their metal tools and at the weapons which fired lethal shots. They must also have been surprised at the powerful effects of the strange liquids which the white people drank. Settlers were happy to trade guns and alcoholic drinks with the Indians in return for furs and foodstuffs. Strong alcoholic drink had a dreadful effect on the Indians, as did the diseases which Europeans brought with them to North America. Guns, too, had their effect. Indians did not usually fight to kill. Their main object, as you will see later, was not to kill but to steal horses or women. Scalping was also spread by European settlers. It was originally done only by the Mohican Indians, but English settlers began to offer money for Indian scalps. Scalping spread to other Indian tribes further inland, along with European diseases, guns, and alcohol.

13 These Hudson Bay fur trappers depended on Indians to guide them round the areas where they were trapping.

The French

In 1607 Jamestown, Virginia, was founded by the English. A year later a Frenchman, Samuel Champlain, claimed lands on the banks of the St Lawrence River for King Henry IV of France. Champlain built a fort where the city of Quebec, in Canada, now stands. France did not intend to be left behind in the European race to claim parts of the New World as their own. Spain had already claimed vast areas in South and Central America. England was setting up colonies along the east coast of North America.

French people were not as eager as the Spanish and the English to sail across the Atlantic to the New World. The Spanish came to Central and South America for gold and silver, fame and fortune, silk and slaves. The English

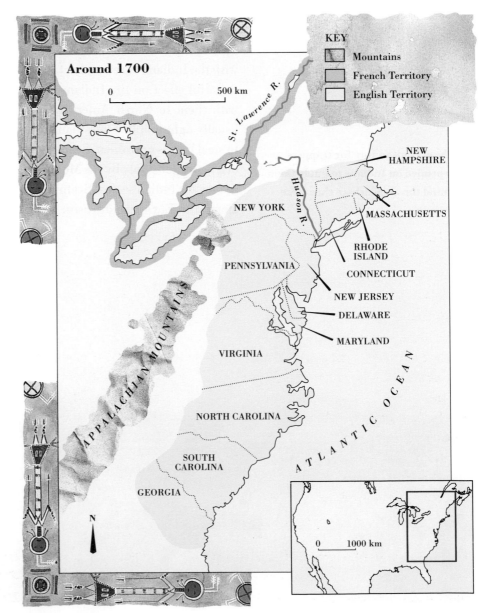

KEY

	Mountains
	French Territory
	English Territory

Around 1700

0   500 km

St. Lawrence R.

Hudson R.

NEW HAMPSHIRE

NEW YORK

MASSACHUSETTS

RHODE ISLAND

PENNSYLVANIA

CONNECTICUT

NEW JERSEY

DELAWARE

MARYLAND

VIRGINIA

APPALACHIAN MOUNTAINS

ATLANTIC OCEAN

NORTH CAROLINA

SOUTH CAROLINA

GEORGIA

N

0   1000 km

14 The areas settled by the French and the English by 1715.

settled in North America mainly in order to farm. No one had, as yet, found any gold or silver in North America. Farming was more difficult in 'New France' than in 'New England' and the winters were colder. So the French came to trap and to trade fur, which would make them very rich.

Indians and the French

The French traders and trappers were bold and fearless. They went deep into the forests surrounding the Great Lakes. They shared the Indians' way of life. Some married Indian women and wore Indian dress. In this way they explored and mapped the lands in North America from Hudson bay in the North to New Orleans in the south. They found and sailed down the Mississippi River. French traders even ventured westwards beyond the Mississippi.

Some French explorers, however, didn't think too highly of the Indians. Colonel Bougainville, of the French army, wrote this to his brother in France:

15 *Indians, naked, black, red, howling, bellowing, dancing, singing the war song, getting drunk, yelling for 'broth' that is to say, blood.*

Colonel Bougainville, letter to his brother, 1750

The Indian tribes of North America, as you have seen, found that their way of life and their lands were being threatened by the English settlers. The French got on much better with the Indians partly because there were fewer of them. It was also because the French came not to farm the land but to hunt and trap. The English chopped down the trees so that they could farm on land which the Indians regarded as theirs. The French moved silently through the forests in search of animals to shoot and trap, not disturbing the Indians at all.

It was not all easy. The Indians who lived in the areas claimed by the French belonged to the Algonquian-speaking group of Indians. They were ancient rivals of the Iroquois Indians. The Algonquians traded furs for guns with the French. With these guns they terrorised the Iroquois. The Iroquois, in turn, obtained guns from the English settlers, determined to settle old grievances once and for all. They set about the Algonquians ferociously. The French took care to avoid the Iroquois hunting grounds. As friends of the Algonquians they might be attacked.

By the end of the eighteenth century the Indians in the eastern parts of North America had been pushed back from their lands by the English and by the French. The French had crushed the Iroquois and the Creek Confederacy of Indians, in the lands just north of Florida, caused no trouble.

Westwards beyond the Mississippi, however, in the vast, untamed Great Plains in the heart of North America, lived the Plains Indians. They had been roaming the Plains, hunting buffalo, untroubled by white people, for centuries. This, as you will see, was soon to change.

1 The French brought the Indians cheap European goods. Was this the main reason for the French getting on well with the Indians? Explain your answer.

Review and Assessment

Look back at all the parts of Chapters 1 and 2 which tell you about the Indians and the European settlers in North America.

1 What changes do you think there would have been in the Indians' ways of life during the fifteenth and sixteenth centuries?

2 Which aspects of their lives do you think would *not* have changed?

3 Some parts of their lives would have changed quickly. Others would have taken more time. Try to suggest some which would have changed *quickly* and some which would have changed *slowly*.

4 The Indians' way of life certainly changed. Do you think that it improved as well as changed? Explain your answer.
Look at sources 11–15. You could also use the text on pages 14–17.

5 Make two lists under these headings:

Why Indians might have welcomed settlers.   *Why Indians might* not *have welcomed settlers.*

6 Now make new lists under these headings:

Why the English settlers wanted to be friendly with the Indians.   *Why the English settlers felt that the Indians were a nuisance.*

Why the French settlers wanted to be friendy with the Indians.   *Why the French settlers felt that the Indians were a nuisance.*

7 Now use the lists which you have made to help you write two accounts:
a An Indian explains his feelings about English *or* French settlers.
b An English *or* a French settler explains his feelings about the Indians in the area in which they have settled.

3 The Plains Indians: beliefs and culture

You read in Chapter 1 how the Indians came to America. You then saw how Europeans in search of spices, riches and new lands explored the lands in which the Indians lived. We are now going to look in detail at the lives of the Plains Indians of North America. Look at the map on pages 6–7. Find the Great Plains, where the Plains Indians lived. For many centuries the Plains Indians were poor tribes, living difficult and dangerous lives. They were often close to starving for lack of food. The Plains were bare and empty, except for the huge herds of buffalo which drifted over the vast, empty spaces, grazing wherever the grass was sweetest. The Indians lived on the fringes of the Great Plains, along the banks of trickling, muddy rivers. They grew maize and beans, and sometimes hunted buffalo when they needed meat. They used to cover themselves with animal skins to disguise their human smell, and crawl along the ground to try to kill buffalo.

This way of life changed quite dramatically when Europeans came to America from the 15th C. Most important, the Spanish brought horses. The Indians had never seen horses before. By the middle of the eighteenth century herds of wild horses had made their way north to the Plains. The Indians realised that they could ride these horses to follow their all-important buffalo across the Great Plains. What was more important, they could now hunt them much more efficiently.

1 Indians, covered in wolf skins, stalk a herd of buffalo. This drawing was made in 1841. George Catlin travelled all over the Plains and spent a lot of time with the Indians.

2 Sioux Indian horses, painted for battle. The Plains Indians looked on their horses as important warriors. They painted them with designs, just as they painted their own bodies.

1 Why did horses make such a difference to the lives of the Plains Indians?

The beliefs of the Plains Indians

The Great Spirit

All Indians believed in the Great Spirit. The Great Spirit ruled over everything and lived in the Happy Hunting Ground, a beautiful country beyond the skies. The Indians' greatest hope was to go to the Happy Hunting Ground when they died. They would only do this if they served the Great Spirit well during their lifetime.

The Plains Indians also believed that all living things had spirits of their own. This meant that they treated humans, animals, birds, fish, insects and plants with the same sort of respect. There was a closeness between man and all natural things – *all* living things were important.

There was, however, more to the Indians' religious beliefs than simply a closeness to nature. This closeness grew from an understanding of the powerful forces which were at work within nature. They believed that the power of the earth always moved and worked in circles. Circles were all around them. The sky was round and so was the sun which shone from it. The wind whirled in circles, and the seasons formed one great circle, always coming back to where they started. Even the life of a person was like a circle. People began as children and ended up, when they were very old, behaving like children again. Birds built round nests and the Plains Indians' own home, the *tipi*, was also round.

The Indians believed that they could only use this power of the earth if they understood the natural world properly. They would never try to interfere with nature. Their aim was to understand the forces which surrounded them. They could then work with these forces and their power would become the Indians' own power.

3 A robe made from buffalo skin and decorated with the sacred circle design.

2 How many different sorts of circles can you find mentioned on these pages? Are there other circles which the Indians might have thought important?

4 The 'medicine wheel' on Medicine Mountain in Wyoming. This was a circle built by the Indians.

1 **Why do you think the Indians gave the months these names? If you could give the months of the year new names, what would you call them? Write down some suggestions. Where your ideas based on nature, like the Indians' names, or on something else?**

Black Elk, a holy man of the Oglala Sioux, described his feelings to a white man, J. Neihardt, who wrote down everything which Black Elk told him:

5 *My friend, I am going to tell you the story of my life. It is the story of all that is holy and good to tell, and of us two leggeds sharing it with the four leggeds and the wings of the air. For these are children of one mother and their father is one spirit.*

J. Neihardt, *Black Elk Speaks*, 1974

Black Elk also gave the names of which Sioux Indians gave to the months:

6
January	*Moon of the Frost in the Tepee*
February	*Moon of the Dark Red Calves*
March	*Moon of the Snow Blind*
April	*Moon of the Red Grass Appearing*
May	*Moon when the Ponies Shed*
June	*Moon of Making Fat*
July	*Moon of the Red Cherries*
August	*Moon when the Cherries turn Black*
September	*Moon when the Calves grow Hair*
October	*Moon of the Changing Season*
November	*Moon of the Falling Leaves*
December	*Moon of the Popping Trees*

Visions

Visions were very important to all Indians. They believed that it was through visions that they could come into contact with the spirits and with the one Great Spirit which flows through the world. Black Elk, of the Oglala Sioux, describes a vision which he had as a child:

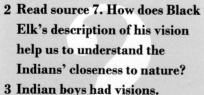
2 **Read source 7. How does Black Elk's description of his vision help us to understand the Indians' closeness to nature?**
3 **Indian boys had visions. Indian girls did not. Does this mean that girls were less important than boys to the Indians? Explain your answer.**

7 *It was when I was five years old that my grandfather made me a bow and some arrows. The grass was young and I was on horseback. A thunderstorm was coming from where the sun goes down, and just as I was riding into the woods along a creek there was a kingbird sitting on a branch. I was going to shoot the kingbird with the bow my grandfather had made, when the bird spoke and said: 'The clouds all over are one sided.' Perhaps it meant that the clouds were looking at me. And then it said: 'Listen! A voice is calling you!' Then I looked at the clouds and two men were coming there, headfirst like arrows slanting down. As they came they sang a sacred song and the thunder was like drumming.*

I sat there gazing at them and they were coming from the place where the giant lives. But when they were close to me they wheeled about towards where the sun goes down, and suddenly they were geese. Then they were gone, and the rain came with a big sound and a roaring.

J. Neihardt, *Black Elk Speaks*, 1974

There was a great feast after a young man had seen his vision. He was then given his adult name. This might be, for example, 'Sitting Bull', 'Grey Raven' or 'Running Water', depending on what he had seen in his vision.

It was different for girls. Indians believed that girls could easily make contact with the spirit world. When a girl began her monthy periods she received the power to talk freely with the spirits. The only problem for the girl was learning how to control these spirits before they controlled her. She was taken away by an old medicine woman who taught her how to control the spirits. She then returned to her tribe and her family. She was given her adult name and there was a great feast to celebrate this.

Medicine men

The medicine man was important because he explained the meaning of young people's visions. This was not the only work he had to do for a tribe. He made contact with the spirits of all living things. It was this which made it possible for him to explain visions. Since he could make contact with the spirits, Indians believed that he had the power to cure illness.

Each male Indian had his own 'medicine'. This was a collection of objects which were very important to him, like a bird's claw or a flower. These might have something to do with his vision. The medicine man would help him to understand this, and to know what to put in the small bag which he always wore round his neck. He told no one but the medicine man what was in his bag. When he died it was buried with him. Girls and squaws did not need a medicine bag. They had all the power which they needed because they could so easily make contact with the spirit world.

8 **A painting on an animal skin showing an Apache girl's puberty ceremony.**

9 *Young men go up on to a hill, and cry and pray for some animal or bird to come to them. For five or six days they neither eat nor drink, and they become thin. While in this state they dream, and whatever animal or bird they see in their dreams becomes their medicine and guardian through life. They are also told in a dream what description of herbs or roots to gather as their medicine, and this they collect and put carefully into a small bag as a charm. They also kill the animal they dreamed of and keep its skin as a charm. No one knows what is the medicine which they have gathered; it is kept a secret. The little bag is kept in the tent, and no one may touch it but the owner.*

J. G. Frazer, *The Native Races of America*, 1939

11 George Catlin drew this picture of a Blackfoot medicine man in the 1830s. He is covered by the skin of a yellow bear and has snakes and other animals dangling over him.

10 *An infant's navel cord was cut immediately after birth and put into a small decorated bag that was retained for life, often worn round the neck. This was the individual's personal medicine. Just as the navel cord provided the link beween the baby in the womb and the woman who gave it life, so the medicine acted as a link between the person and the spiritual world. The actual contents of the bundle were known only to the holder. As the owner matured and his spiritual strength became greater, the contents of the bundle were added to. The bundle was buried with the owner when he died.*

M. Campbell, *People of the Buffalo*, 1976

1 Read sources 9 and 10 very carefully. These are two different descriptions of medicine bags and what Indians put into them. They were both written by people who had studied the Plains Indians' way of life in great detail.

a) Copy the following statements about medicine bags. Then, beside each statement put the number of the source(s) (9 or 10 or both 9 and 10) which the idea came from.

  i) Indians owned medicine bags from the moment they were born.

  ii) An Indian boy's navel cord was put into his medicine bag.

  iii) Objects could only be put into a boy's bag after he had had his vision.

  iv) Only the owner knew what was in his medicine bag.

  v) Only the owner ever touched his medicine bag.

b) Why do you think that the sources say different things about medicine bags?

Dances

Medicine men could always make contact with the spirits, and so, at times, could other Indians. When there was great trouble, however, the tribe as a whole needed to make contact with the spirits. Perhaps the buffalo herds had disappeared. Perhaps the river had dried up. When they could not find buffalo, the Indians did not waste time going out and tracking them. They performed complicated dances to try to bring themselves closer to the spirit world. They hoped that in this way they could work with the power of the spirits to bring the buffalo back.

12 A Mandan buffalo dance, drawn by George Catlin in the 1830s.

The Sun Dance was the most important of the Indians' religious ceremonies. The longest sun dances, lasting eight days, were performed by the Cheyenne and the Arapaho Indians. They believed that the more pain the dancers could endure, the more the spirits would look upon the tribe with favour.

Black Elk, an Oglala Sioux, describes a sun dance.

13 *First their bodies were painted by the holy men. Then each would lay down beneath the tree as though he were dead, and the holy man would cut a place in his back or chest, so that a strip of rawhide, fastened to the top of the tree, could be pushed through and tied. Then the man would get up and dance to the drums, leaning on the rawhide strip as long as he could stand the pain or until the flesh tore.*

J. Neihardt, *Black Elk Speaks*, 1974

14 Detail of the sun dance, drawn by Frederic Remington in the 1880s.

2 Which parts of Black Elk's description of a sun dance could you use to describe Frederic Remington's painting?

3 Which do you think would be more useful to us for finding out about the sun dance: Black Elk's description or Frederic Remington's painting? Explain your answer.

4 The Indians believed that dances would help them to contact the spirits. What other ways did they have of making contact with the spirits?

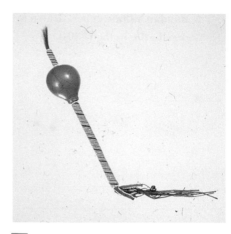

15 Indian Musical instrument: an Arapaho rattle.

Music

The Plains Indians used music on many occasions. There were the songs which young men heard during their visions. There were songs sung by spirit helpers in dreams to help at difficult times. There were songs sung during dances like the sun dance or the buffalo dance. These songs were accompanied by drums made from buffalo hide stretched over a wooden frame and beaten with padded wooden sticks. Some tribes played a simple wind instrument, the *flageolet*. This was quite like a modern recorder.

George Catlin describes Sioux music:

16 *The musical instruments used amongst these people are few . . . consisting chiefly of rattles, drums, whistles and lutes, all of which are used in the different tribes.*

It has been said by some travellers, that the Indian has neither harmony or melody in his music . . . for the most part of their vocal exercises [singing] *there is a total absence of what the musical world would call melody; their songs being made up chiefly of a sort of violent chant of harsh and jarring gutterals, of yelps, barks and screams, which are given out in perfect time. . .*

George Catlin, *Manners, Customs and Conditions of the North American Indians*, 1844

17 The music and words for the Sioux rabbit dance, written down in conventional musical notation by an expert on the music of the American Indians.

1 If you are able to read music, have a close look at the rabbit dance. It has been made to look like the sort of music which we use, but would it sound like anything which we are used to? If you can't read music, see if your music teacher will play or sing this for you.

4 Hunting and warfare

The buffalo

Hunting the buffalo

As soon as they had horses, the Plains Indians did not have to stalk the buffalo on foot. They could now hunt the buffalo on horseback in a thrilling and skilful chase.

1 'The Buffalo Hunt', 1844, by George Catlin.

A scientist who lived with the Indians for a while took part in a buffalo hunt in 1872. He later wrote:

> **2** *It is sad to see so much death, but the people must have food, and none of the meat would be wasted.*

George Grinnell, *When the Buffalo Ran*, 1920

Nothing, indeed, was wasted. The buffalo supplied nearly everything which the Indians needed. These animals were so important to the Plains Indians that Francis Parkman, who made a journey through Indian country in the 1840s, wrote in his book, *The Oregon Trail*, that 'When the buffalo are extinct, the Indian too must dwindle away'.

Using the buffalo

When the hunters had brought the buffalo back to camp, the women used to cut out the parts which were good to eat raw, like the kidneys, the liver and the brain. They boiled or roasted the flesh before they ate it. They sliced anything which was left over into thin strips which they smoked or dried in the sun. This 'jerky', as it was called, used to keep for a long time. It would help to feed the tribe during the cold winter months. The women also made 'pemmican' from left-over meat. To do this they pounded the meat until it was pulp, mixed it with berries and poured it into skin containers. They poured hot grease and marrowfat over this to make the container airtight. The pemmican would then keep for a very long time. Black Elk describes what happened back in camp after a buffalo hunt by the Oglala Sioux.

> **3** *Women back at the camp were cutting long poles and forked sticks to make drying racks for the meat. When the hunters got home they threw their meat in piles on the leaves of trees. The women were all busy cutting the red meat into strips and hanging it on the racks to dry. You could see the red meat hanging everywhere. The people feasted all night long and danced and sang.*

J. Neihardt, *Black Elk Speaks*, 1974

You can see from the drawing that the Indians used the buffalo for many things, not just food. The one part which was not used was the heart. This did not mean that it was not important. It was cut from the dead animal and left on the Plains to give new life to the herd which had given the Indians their much-needed buffalo.

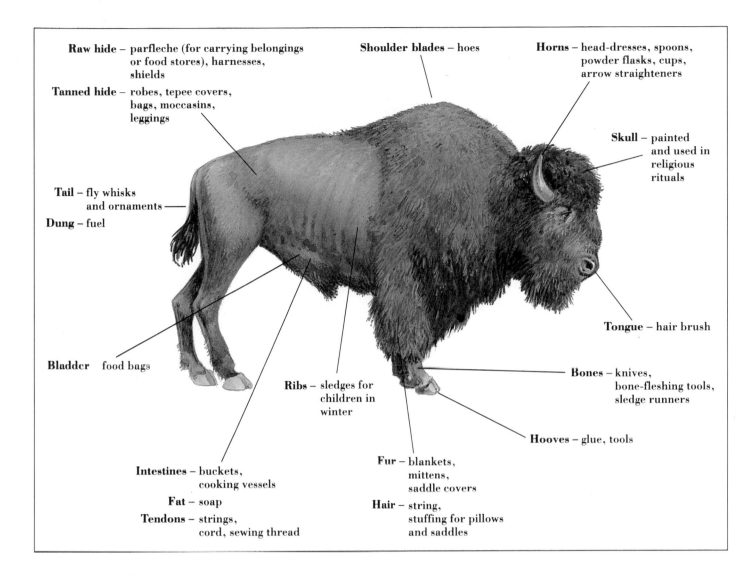

4 This picture shows how the Indians used all the different parts of the buffalo.

Warfare

5 *You may go on the warpath.*
When your name I hear,
Having done something brave
Then I will marry you.

Sioux Love Song

Every young Indian boy dreamed of winning glory in war. No man could be respected or become a chief until he had shown that he was a brave and successful fighter.

Indian ideas about going to war were quite different from those of white people. Indian warfare was made up of short raids by small groups to capture horses or kill their enemies. White people, at that time, went to war to conquer other people or to gain land.

An Indian band's wealth did not depend on the amount of land which it had. Indians did not believe that anyone could own land. Their riches were the horses which they owned or had stolen from other tribes.

The Plains Indians were marvellous riders. George Catlin was amazed by their skill:

> **6** *The Comanche are the most extraordinary horsemen that I have ever seen in all my travels. A Comanche on his feet is awkward as a monkey on the ground, but the moment he lays his hand upon his horse his face even becomes handsome, and he gracefully flies away like a different being.*
>
> George Catlin, *Manners, Customs and Conditions of the North American Indians*, 1844

Games

7 A game very like lacrosse, played by the Sioux. The painting was made by Seth Eastman in 1852.

Indians enjoyed playing games. This helped them to develop the skills and strength which they needed for warfare. The painting shows Indians playing a game very much like our modern game of lacrosse.

Counting coup

The Plains Indians would not have understood the way in which white men fought battles. The white man thought that he should stand and fight until the last man was dead. The Indian gained his greatest honour when he touched his enemy, dead or alive, with his 'coup stick'. This was known as 'counting coup'. A white man would have felt that this showed no bravery at all. An Indian warrior did not want to die. What a waste that would be! Why risk being killed when he could slip away and live to fight another day?

Counting coup by touching the enemy with your hand or with a specially decorated stick was the highest honour which a warrior could win, especially if his enemy was alive. He had been amongst the enemy and had come back alive! The first man to touch an enemy in this way received the highest honour. There were lesser honours for those who touched the enemy second, third or fourth.

A warrior's success in warfare depended on how many times he had counted coup. A famous Crow chief had counted coup so many times that he was known as Plenty Coup! Successful warriors could be spotted immediately by the feathers which they wore on their heads.

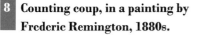

8 Counting coup, in a painting by Frederic Remington, 1880s.

9 The meaning of different feathers.

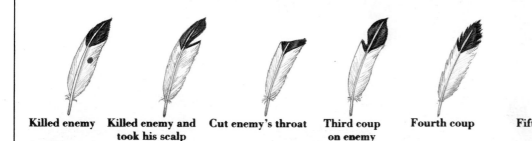

| Killed enemy | Killed enemy and took his scalp | Cut enemy's throat | Third coup on enemy | Fourth coup | Fifth coup | Wearer wounded many times |

Scalping

You read on page 15 that the Mohican Indians' custom of scalping their enemies spread to other Indians when European settlers began to offer money for Indian scalps. Fear of being scalped was a very good reason for the Indians' wish not to be killed in battle. Being scalped was one of the very worst things which could happen to an Indian. If your enemy had your scalp, he also had your spirit. This would prevent you from going to the Happy Hunting Ground. For the same reason Indians would be very careful when cutting their hair or their nails. They would always bury the cuttings secretly in case anyone found them and gained hold of their spirit.

When an Indian killed someone in battle, he scalped the person and carried the scalp back to camp. Indians used to dry the scalps and display them on top of *tipi* poles. After a successful raid the tribe used to do a scalp dance. Warriors and their squaws used to dance and sing around the scalps which they had brought back.

10 **A scalp dance, painted by George Catlin in 1840.**

Weapons

The white man brought the Indians the horses which changed their lives. He also brought guns. Indians who got hold of these became even deadlier shots than they already were with bows and arrows. Indians still used their traditional weapons, though. You can see some of these here.

1 Which of these actions would an Indian have thought to be brave? Use the sources in this chapter as well as what you have learned about the Plains Indians to help you to explain your answers.
   a) When the last arrow had been fired. Wild Crow galloped furiously into the enemy camp. He touched Chief Still Waters with his coup stick as the chief lay dead in front of his *tipi*.
   b) The Cheyenne were attacking! The band prepared to leave their *tipis* and go to the hills for safety. Grey Raven refused to go with them. He fought the Cheyenne until he was killed defending his own *tipi*.
   c) Black Eagle slid into the enemy camp late at night. He trod silently until he reached the *tipi* of Chief Hard Foot. Carefully he cut the hide rope which bound the horses to the sleeping men inside, and made off with his prizes.

2 Which sources did you use to help you make up your mind?

3 Which of these actions, a), b) or c), do *you* think to be brave?
   Are your ideas of bravery the same as the Indians'? Why do you think this is?

4 Which do you think were more important to the Plains Indians – horses or buffalo? Use all the sources and what you have read in this chapter to help you to explain your anwser.

11 A traditional Indian weapon and a warrior's shield.

5 Family life

The *tipi*

You can see what a *tipi* looked like in the photograph. You have read a description of a *tipi*. You can also see how Indians moved in the photograph of the *travois*.

Put together a plan for designing and constructing a *tipi*. Bear in mind it must:

a) be made from buffalo hide;

b) be able to be put up and taken down quickly and easily;

c) be waterproof (only natural materials were available then – no waterproof sprays!);

d) enable smoke from the fire to go out of the top, depending on the direction of the wind;

e) be as draught-proof as possible;

f) be stable in windy weather (no guy lines and pegs allowed);

g) be able to be carried around without wheeled transport;

h) be big enough to house more than one family.

The buffalo also provided the Plains Indians with their homes. The *tipi* was the home of each Indian family. It was a tent with a frame of wooden poles arranged in a circle and covered with between ten and twenty buffalo hides, sewn together.

In winter, a fire in the middle of the *tipi* helped to keep the family warm and cook their food. The smoke from the fire went out through a hole in the top. There were flags which the Indians adjusted according to the direction of the wind, so that the smoke could blow away. They decorated their *tipis* inside and out with brightly coloured paintings of animals and birds, or with geometric designs. They put rugs on the floor. On top of these they put comfortable cushions made of skins and stuffed with a soft filling.

A white man who travelled for many years among the Plains Indians, wrote about the *tipi*:

> **1** *In this small space are often crowded eight or ten persons, possibly of three or four different families. Since the cooking, eating, living and sleeping are all done in the one room, it soon becomes inconceivably [unbelievably] filthy.*

Colonel Dodge, *Hunting Grounds of the Great West*, 1877

Chief Flying Hawk, of the Oglala Sioux, did not agree with him. 'The *tipi* is always clean, warm in winter, cool in summer,' he said.

It is, perhaps, not surprising that Colonel Dodge was just a little critical of the *tipi*. He did go on to admire its design, but life in a *tipi* must have seemed strange to someone used to living in a house.

Indians on the move

The Plains Indians needed to follow the herds of buffalo which roamed the plains. So they had to take down their *tipis* quite frequently and put them up again somewhere else. When they moved camp they had to take everything with them. They used *travois* to carry all their possessions. These were made from two *tipi* poles, joined at the horse's shoulders. The other ends trailed along the ground. In the middle of the poles they put a frame or net for carrying their belongings – and small children and puppies!

2 Shoshoni Chief Washakie's village in Wyoming. This photograph was taken in September 1870.

3 Gros Ventre women moving camp with *travois*. This photograph was taken towards the end of the nineteenth century.

Family life

Bands, tribes and nations

Indian families, as you have seen, lived in *tipis*. Sometimes, several families shared a *tipi*. All families which were related to each other used to put up their *tipis* close together and travel in a group called a band. All the different bands in a tribe usually met together in the summer for a great tribal camp. This took place when the grass was rich enough to feed all the buffalo which they needed for their camp. Some tribes were part of a larger group called a nation. The Oglala Sioux and Teton Sioux, for example, were both part of the Sioux nation. This diagram shows you how a nation was split into tribes and bands.

4 The Sioux Nation.

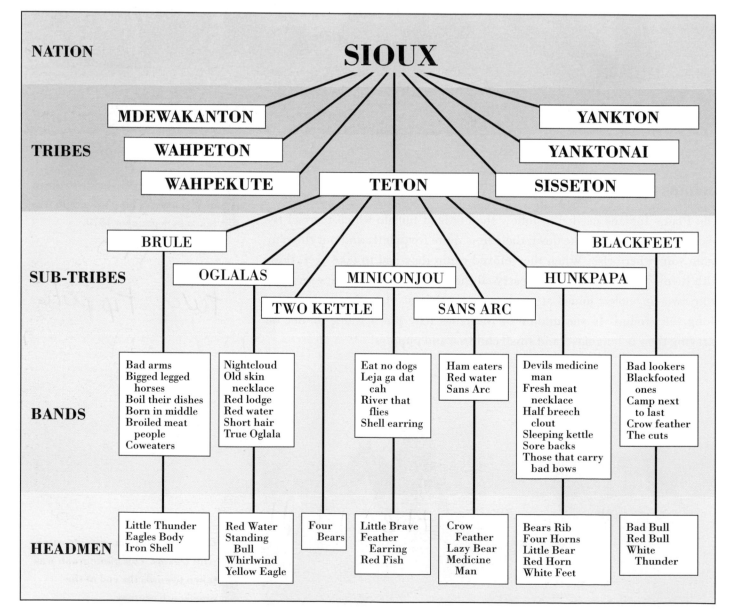

1 Look at the picture of the Comanche village. Why do you think they put their *tipis* so close together?

Children

Francis Parkman once stayed with the Oglala Sioux Chief Big Crow and his family. He wrote this about the family.

> 5 *Both he and his squaw, like most other Indians, were very fond of their children, whom they never punished except in extreme cases, when they threw a bowl of cold water over them.*

Francis Parkman, *The Oregon Trial*, 1840

The Indian way of bringing up children was very different from the way in which Francis Parkman had been brought up. Indian parents did not often punish their children. They taught them, from a very early age, to respect all living things. The mother earth and everything which lived on her had to be respected. For this reason parents did not ill-treat their children, but they also made sure that their children treated their elders with respect at all times.

All members of the family were important to each other. Since they lived in a band in which most of the people were related to each other, children were never without someone to look after them. Indian children didn't call their parents, brothers and sisters 'auntie' and 'uncle' as we do. They called them 'mother' and 'father'. They also treated their cousins as if they were their brothers and sisters.

6 George Catlin's painting of a Comanche village in the 1830s.

The survival of the tribe was the most important thing and often difficult choices had to be taken as this source suggests.

> **7** *A squaw with three small children was also left. She carried one on her back and another in her arms, while the eldest trotted along by her side. Some time after, a young Indian who had loitered behind came up and reported that the squaw had just killed the youngest because it was too small to travel.*
>
> Adapted from H. A. Boller, *Among the Indians: Eight Years in the Far West*, 1972

Braves and squaws

As children got older, their families prepared them for the different parts which they would have to play when they were adults. A boy learned the skills of a warrior like riding a horse and how to fight. A girl learned how to put up and take down a *tipi*, and how to cut up and prepare buffalo to provide food and clothing.

Many tribes believed that the jobs of the men and the women were equally important. Men defended the band against enemies and the women looked after day-to-day living. The women put up and took down the *tipi*, and made sure that this and all the family's possessions were loaded onto the *travois* when they moved camp. The women also prepared the buffalo to make food and clothes.

8 **A young Indian boy learning how to break in a pony (woodcut by Frederic Remington).**

Not all Indian marriages were happy. 'I throw her away!' Simply by beating a drum and shouting these words a Cheyenne could divorce his wife. The problem was that, in many tribes, everything – *tipi*, utensils, tools, children – belonged to the women. When a man from one of these tribes wanted to divorce his wife, he had to leave everything except the clothes he was wearing and go back to his mother's *tipi*.

Widows and old people

The Plains Indians had to depend on the strength of the band to protect them against their enemies. They had to think of the safety of the whole band as well as of the people within it. As a result, the Indians had some customs which seem strange to us today.

If men were killed in hunting or in war, their widows were shared out and married to the surviving men, even if they had wives already. This helped the women as well as the men, since one wife could not always do everything necessary for a growing family on the move. This also made sure that all women could have as many children as possible. In this way the tribe increased in numbers and strength.

Old people were a big problem to tribes which were always on the move. They became too ill or too weak to keep up with the band. Many old Indians used to go off by themselves to die so that they would not be a nuisance to the band when it moved on.

George Catlin describes the way in which an old Indian decided that his band should go on without him:

9 *'My children,' said he, 'our nation is poor, and it is necessary that you should go to the country where you can get meat. My strength is no more, my days are numbered, and I am a burden to my children. I cannot go, and wish to die.'*

George Catlin, *Manners, Customs and Conditions of the North American Indians*, 1844

1 Read source 7. As you have read, Indians loved their children very much. Why, then, did this squaw kill her youngest child?

2 Read source 9. Do you think that the old man's family should have persuaded him to carry on with them? Explain your answer.

Indian Clothes

Indian men and women did not wear the same sort of clothes for day-to-day living and for important occasions. They made most of their clothes out of the skins of animals which they killed. They also wore clothes and blankets made of cloth which they had got from white Americans. For special occasions however, they wore beautifully decorated clothes which they made themselves. The pictures on these pages show just how skilful they were. See how clever they were at bead-work and how they used feathers. Imagine the skill needed to make the deer-skin dress and the jacket.

10 An Indian man's beaded jacket.

11 A woman's dress, made from two soft deerskins sewn together and decorated with beads.

12 A Sioux Indian head-dress, dating from 1880.

How did the Indians keep law and order?

Indians did not generally need to keep law and order. Everything was controlled by custom and tradition. Indians hated to do wrong, because if they did, they would be badly thought of and shamed in public.

1 The Cheyenne Dog Soldiers were very important. People listened to what they said and took their advice. Why do you think this was so? (Clue: look back at the section on the buffalo on pages 27–28).

2 Look back at pages 38–39, which suggest that women had an important part to play in the life of the tribe. Why do you think there were no squaws on the Indian councils?

14 An Indian Council, painted by Seth Eastman in 1849. Eastman was a US army officer who made over 300 paintings of Indian people.

The little government that was needed by the tribe was mainly in the hands of a Council of leading men from each band. These were usually peace chiefs. In some tribes there were different chiefs for peace and for war. Chiefs did not, however, give orders to their people. They offered advice, and Indians did not necessarily listen to their chief any more than to any other respected member of their band or tribe. The Council could not make any decisions until every member had agreed. During these meetings of the Council that the ceremonial smoking of a pipe took place. The Indians believed that the smoke would carry their words and their wishes up into the spirit world. The spirits would then help the members of the Council to make wise decisions.

Warrior societies

Each tribe had its own warrior societies and each man belonged to one. Every warrior society had its own special costume, dances and songs. One of the most famous societies was the Dog Soldiers of the Cheyenne. Their job was to protect the tribe. They also had to protect the buffalo:

13 *One of the most important functions of the 'Dog Soldiers' is the protection of game* [animals to be killed for food]. *Except when laying in the supply of meat for the winter, only sufficient buffalo is killed for the current supply of the camp. Great care is taken not to alarm the herd, which will feed for days around a camp of a thousand people, while half a dozen white men would have driven them away.*

Colonel Dodge, *Hunting Grounds of the Great West*, 1877

Review and Assessment

1 Look at source 2 on page 35. What does this picture tell you about the Plains Indians?

2 Why was the buffalo so important to the Plains Indians? Use sources 3 and 4 (Chapter 4) and source 13 (Chapter 5), as well as what you have read in Chapter 4, to help you to write your answer.

3 Some sources give more useful evidence than others. Choose one source you used for answering Questions 1 and 2 which you feel is most useful for telling you about the Plains Indians' way of life.
a Why did you choose this source?
b Why do you feel that it is more useful than all the others for telling you about the Plains Indians?

4 Read source 1 and also what Flying Hawk said (page 34). Which of the two sources do you think is more reliable about what *tipis* were like? Explain your answer.

5 Read again the source which, in your answer to Question 4, you did *not* think gave reliable evidence about the *tipi*. Is this source useful as evidence for anything else?

6 'The Indians were cruel, bloodthirsty and uncivilised. They left old people and babies to die. They made men dance with rawhide strips through their chests. They scalped their enemies.'
a This is one person's view of the Plains Indians. Which sources in Chapters 3, 4 and 5 did they use to come to this conculsion?
b Now write a *different* interpretation of the Plains Indians. Use *only* these sources: Chapter 3, sources 5 and 6; Chapter 4, source 6; Chapter 5, sources 5 and 10–12.
c Why is your interpretation different from the first one?
d Is yours more accurate than this?
e What other reasons might there be for people saying different things about the Plains Indians?

6 People move west

For a long time only the Indians lived on the Plains, but by the beginning of the nineteenth century many people who lived in the east of North America were beginning to explore the rest of the country which lay west of the Appalachian Mountains. The Appalachian Mountains rose to heights of 2000 metres, with steep rock faces and deep valleys. The Mississippi River was wide, slow and dangerous. Beyond this came the prairie grasslands and the Great Plains. The Plains were empty and dry, with sudden storms, scorching sun and droughts. They stretched for hundreds of kilometres to the foothills of the Rocky Mountains. The Rockies were over 1000 kilometres wide and reached heights of over 5000 metres. They had deep ravines and high mountain passes which were completely blocked with snow for months every winter. Even in the summer they were almost impossible to use.

It seemed that the Indians might be the only people who were able to live on the Plains. A lawyer from Vermont (a state on the east coast of North America), travelling from Illinois, near the Mississippi, to Oregon, on the west coast, wrote that the Great Plains region was:

> **1** *burnt and a desert, whose solemn stillness is seldom broken by the tread of any other animal, than the wolf or the starved and thirsty horse which bears the traveler across its wastes.*
>
> Thomas J. Farnham, diary entry, 1839

This did not, however, stop people from exploring and settling in new lands west of the original thirteen states. You can see on the map (source 2) how the United States of America grew bigger and bigger between 1783 and 1853 as the government bought or won more lands.

1 **Why did white Americans believe that no one would ever settle on the Great Plains? Try to think of as many reasons as you can.**

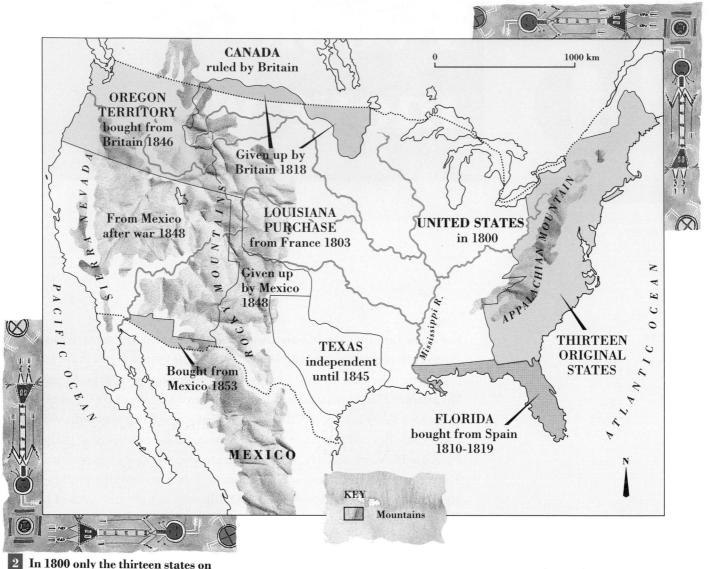

CANADA
ruled by Britain

0   1000 km

OREGON
TERRITORY
bought from
Britain 1846

Given up by
Britain 1818

SIERRA NEVADA

From Mexico
after war 1848

LOUISIANA
PURCHASE
from France 1803

UNITED STATES
in 1800

ROCKY MOUNTAINS

Given up
by Mexico
1848

APPALACHIAN MOUNTAIN

PACIFIC OCEAN

Bought from
Mexico 1853

TEXAS
independent
until 1845

THIRTEEN
ORIGINAL
STATES

Mississippi R.

ATLANTIC OCEAN

FLORIDA
bought from Spain
1810-1819

MEXICO

N

KEY

Mountains

2 In 1800 only the thirteen states on this map formed the United States of America. Thirty years earlier these states had been colonies belonging to Great Britain. Between 1776 and 1783 the thirteen colonies fought Britain and gained their independence. They became the first American states. Then people moved west and settled in the lands between the Appalachian Mountains and the Mississippi. In 1803 the United States government bought vast areas of land from France. These lands included the Great Plains.

3 In 1804 the President of the United States sent two explorers, Meriwether Lewis and William Clark, to explore the lands which the United States had bought from France. They reached the Pacific Coast, but the journey was difficult and dangerous. This drawing shows Lewis and Clark on their expedition.

The early settlers

Mountain men

4 'I took ye for an Injun.'

In 1890 Frederic Remington drew this picture of two mountain men. He added the caption, 'I took ye for an Injun.' It is easy to see why. The mountain man on the right does look very much like one of the Indians you have been reading about in Chapter 4. Mountain men were expert hunters and trackers. Their job was to trap animals for trading companies like the Rocky Mountain Fur Company. They roamed the Sierra Nevada and the Rocky Mountains and saw the fertile plains and rich soils of Oregon and California beyond the Rockies. Some of them married Indian women. Like the Indians, the mountain men knew about the ways of animals and how to use plants. Sometimes they worked with Indians, sometimes they fought them. A mountain man tells here of one occasion when things went badly wrong:

5 *We were completely surrounded. We cocked our rifles and started thro' their ranks which seemed completely filled with Blackfeet. An arrow struck White on the right hip joint. I hastily told him to pull it out and as I spoke another arrow struck me in the same place. . . I kept hopping from log to log thro' a shower of arrows.*

Osborne Russell, diary, 1834–43

Look at Remington's engraving 'I took ye for an Injun' and read sources 5 and 6.

1 It seems that the mountain men did not really trust the Indians. Why, then, did they want to look like them?

2 Read sources 5 and 6. Do you think that the mountain men needed the Indians to be friendly with them more than the Indians needed the mountain men to be friendly with them?

3 These sources seem to give very different ideas of the ways in which mountain men and Indians behaved towards each other. Here are some suggestions to explain these differences. a) Osborne Russell had changed his ideas about Indians between writing the two accounts. b) The and the Blackfeet were not. c) One of the sources is wrong. Is any one of these right – or can you suggest another reason?

It was not always like this. The same man tells of another, different occasion.

6 *I cast my eyes down the mountain and discovered two Indians approaching within 200 yards of us. I immediately roused my companion, who was still sleeping. We grasped our guns. They* [the Indians] *quickly accosted us in the Snake tongue saying they were Shoshoni and friend to the whites. I invited them to approach and sit down, and then gave them some meat and tobacco. After our visitors had eaten and smoked, they pointed out the place where we could descend the mountain.*

Osborne Russell, diary, 1834–43

Pioneers, Mormons and miners

7 **When people travelled west they usually put all their belongings – and the whole family – in wagons like this.**

Between 1839 and the end of the 1850s, thousands of men, women and children left their homes in the east to go west. They packed what they needed into wagons and hand-carts. It was a difficult and dangerous journey across land which they did not know. Many of them wanted to own land to grow crops and raise cattle, but land was scarce in the east and too many people wanted it.

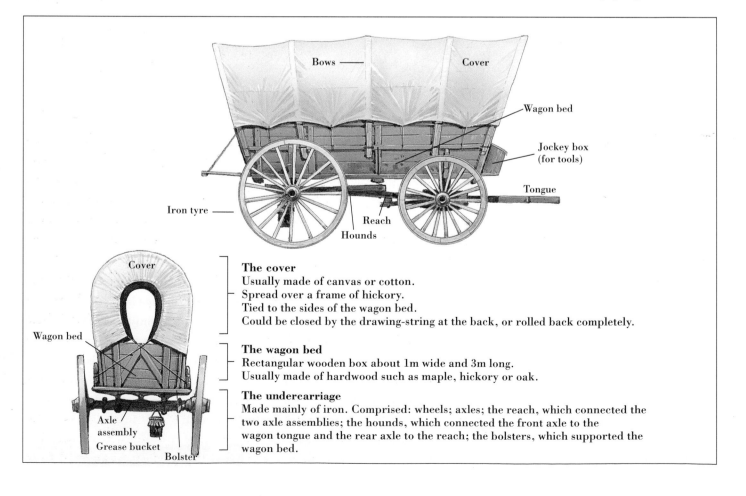

Bows —— Cover

Wagon bed

Jockey box (for tools)

Tongue

Iron tyre ——

Reach
Hounds

Cover

Wagon bed

Axle assembly
Grease bucket
Bolster

The cover
Usually made of canvas or cotton.
Spread over a frame of hickory.
Tied to the sides of the wagon bed.
Could be closed by the drawing-string at the back, or rolled back completely.

The wagon bed
Rectangular wooden box about 1m wide and 3m long.
Usually made of hardwood such as maple, hickory or oak.

The undercarriage
Made mainly of iron. Comprised: wheels; axles; the reach, which connected the two axle assemblies; the hounds, which connected the front axle to the wagon tongue and the rear axle to the reach; the bolsters, which supported the wagon bed.

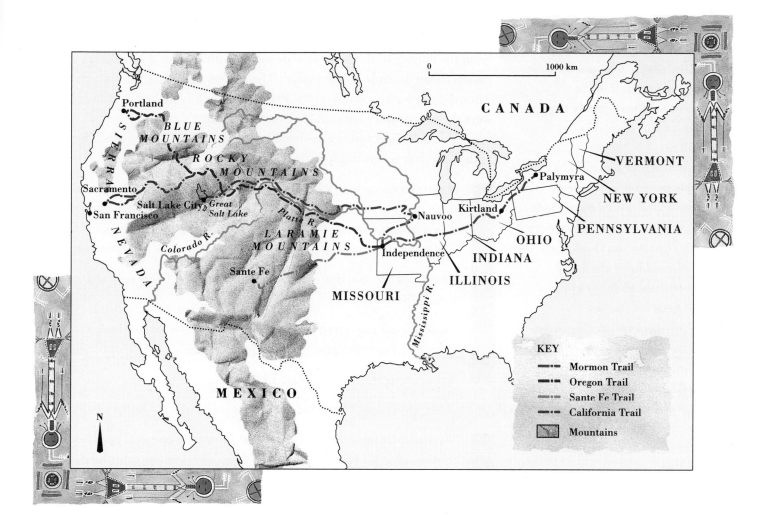

8 **Pioneer trails and the Mormon route.**

Stories of the fertile and empty lands in Oregon and California which mountain men and traders had told, made many look in the far west. Soon so many people travelled west that well-worn trails were made, as you can see on the map. The journeys were not easy. They faced bad weather, disease, hunger and thirst and, sometimes, hostile Indians. Often, though, Indians acted as guides and sheltered people in their villages. After all, these people were not settling on their lands in the Plains.

There were other people who had quite different reasons for travelling the long, difficult journey over to the west. A religious group known as Mormons wanted to be free to live and to worship in their own way. They had beliefs which were different from other Christians, and did not always get on well with them. In the end the Mormons settled in the Great Salt Lake Valley.

Land was not the only reason why people travelled west. Gold was discovered in California in 1848. Quickly, news reached the eastern states – and the rest of the world! Within a few months, 40,000 people crossed the Great Plains. Dozens of ships left ports, bound for California and carrying would-be-miners. Most of them did not find any gold, and wandered back

Read what it says in this Chapter about the people who moved west during the first half of the nineteenth century. Study the sources on this page very carefully.

1 What different reasons did people have for going west?

2 Moving west would have made a lot of difference to everyone's lives. How do you think their lives would have changed?

3 Would these changes always have been for the best?

4 Did the pioneers, the Mormons and the miners have any reasons in common for wanting to go west?

5 What different feelings do you think they would have during the journey and when they arrived?

home. Some did strike gold and became very rich indeed. Then, in the 1850s, people found gold further east, in Colorado. This did not last for very long. Soon the mining settlements were deserted, with broken-down shacks and no miners. They became 'ghost towns'. The miners had come only for the gold. They did not want to settle on the Plains. It certainly looked as if the Indians were the only people who could live on the Plains.

Amelia Knight and her husband left Iowa in 1853 for Oregon. They took with them their seven children.

9 *We are creeping along slowly, one wagon after another . . . and the same thing over, out of one mud hole and into another all day long. The men and boys are all soaking wet and look sad and comfortless. The little ones and myself are shut up in the wagon from the rain.*

Chatfield [her son] quite sick with scarlet fever. A calf took sick and died before breakfast.

I was sick all night and not able to get out of the wagon in the morning. Yesterday my eighth child was born.

Amelia Knight, diary extracts, 1853

One farmer who reached Oregon in 1844 had good news for his family at home.

10 *We had a tedious and tiring trip: but I think we are well paid for our trouble: we are in the best country I have ever seen for farming and stock raising. The prairies are easily broken with oxen. All springs and streams are cool and fine flavoured.*

Nathaniel Ford, letter, 1844

Cattlemen and cowboys

As you have seen, in the early years of the nineteenth century, people travelling west did not really affect the Indians' way of life. But these people did not settle or work on the Plains.

What about the cattlemen and cowboys who did live and work on the Plains? Cattlemen owned the cattle which the cowboys looked after. Texas was the place where the cattlemen first bred cattle. Cowboys used to drive the cattle north to be sold in the markets of the big towns north of Texas. Later on cattlemen were able to take and sell their cattle were taken and sold to buyers in all the states as you can see on the map. This was made possible in the late 1860s, with the building of a railroad which, for the first time, joined the east with the west.

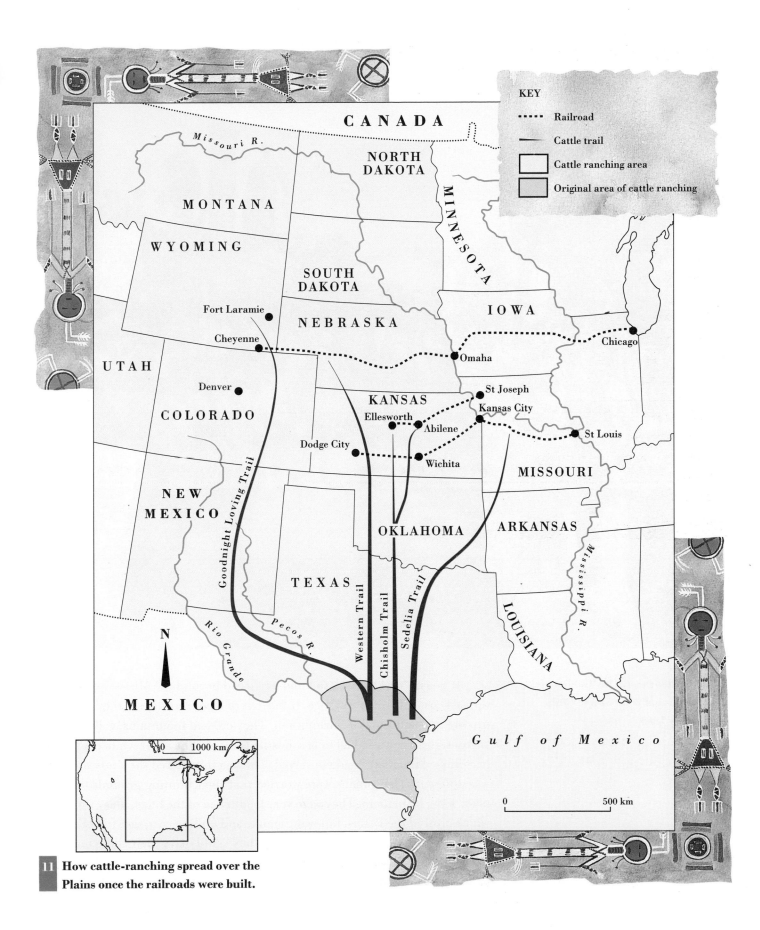

KEY

---- Railroad

——— Cattle trail

☐ Cattle ranching area

▨ Original area of cattle ranching

Missouri R.

NORTH DAKOTA

MONTANA

MINNESOTA

WYOMING

SOUTH DAKOTA

IOWA

Fort Laramie ●

NEBRASKA

Cheyenne ●

Chicago ●

Omaha ●

UTAH

Denver ●

St Joseph ●

KANSAS

Kansas City ●

COLORADO

Ellesworth ●

Abilene ●

St Louis ●

Dodge City ●

Wichita ●

MISSOURI

NEW MEXICO

Goodnight Loving Trail

OKLAHOMA

ARKANSAS

Mississippi R.

N

Rio Grande

Pecos R.

Western Trail

Chisholm Trail

Sedelia Trail

TEXAS

LOUISIANA

MEXICO

Gulf of Mexico

0   1000 km

0   500 km

11 **How cattle-ranching spread over the Plains once the railroads were built.**

12 Railroads meet! The 'Golden Spike' ceremony, Promontary, Utah, 10 May 1869

It was not an easy task to build a railroad beyond the Mississippi to reach the east coast of North America. Hundreds of labourers died as they worked in driving rain and snow or burning sun. They crossed mountains, valleys, rivers and deserts. They also had to face hostile Indians. The other white people who had crossed the Plains had not stayed. They hadn't altered the landscape. This was different. The Indians were worried that their hunting grounds might be taken away from them. They were very frightened of the huge, noisy iron horse which crossed the Plains, billowing smoke and pulling carriages full of people.

Cattlemen in Texas realised that if they could drive their cattle north to a town on the railroad (known as the 'railhead') they could then use the railroad to reach the rapidly growing towns of the mid-west. Soon cattlemen were blazing new trails north to meet up with the railroads. They sold their cattle and became rich. This did not last for very long. The railroads made it easier for people to move onto the Plains to settle and farm the lands. Their farms began to block the cattle trails. The Indians, too, began to make life difficult for the cattlemen and cowboys. They started to make the cowboys pay to drive the cattle over Indian lands. The cattlemen began to think that it would be easier to raise their cattle on the Plains than to drive them there. They began to set up ranches on the Plains and their cattle began to roam freely over the wide open spaces – the 'open range'.

As far as 'cowboys and Indians' are concerned, did they really spend all their time fighting as they do in cowboy films? Look at the sources on the next page and decide for yourself!

14 *The wild ones* [Indians] *would stampede our horses and try to get away with them. The friendly ones would run off with them at night and come back the next day to get a reward for returning them.*

Bill Poage, a 'trail boss', talking about Indians

13 **Photograph of a cowboy in the 1880s**

Days in the life of a cowboy driving a herd of 1000 cattle from Texas to Iowa:

15

8 May   Rain pouring down in torrents. Ran my horse into a ditch and got my knee badly sprained.

14 May   Swam river with rope and then hauled wagon over. Lost most of our kitchen furniture such as camp kettles, coffee pots, cups etc.

1 June   Stampede last night . . . and general mix up and loss of beeves [cattle]. *Hunt cattle again. Men tired and want to leave.*

2 June   Hard rain and wind storm. Beeves ran and I had to be on horseback all night. Awful night. Men still lost. Quit the beeves and go hunting men is the word – 4 p.m. Found our men with Indian guide and 195 beeves 14 miles from camp. Almost starved not having had a bite to eat for 60 hours.

19 June   15 Indians came to herd and tried to take some beeves. Would not let them.

George Duffield, diary entries, 1866

16 *The daily life of a cowboy is one of considerable daily danger and excitement. He lives hard, works hard, has but few comforts and fewer necessities. His life borders nearly on that of an Indian.*

J. G. McCoy, *Historic Sketches of the Cattle Trade of the West and Southwest*, 1874

17 Cowboys shooting at Indians, in a painting made by Frederic Remington in the 1880s.

1 Read these statements. Which ones are *facts* and which are *points of view?*

   a) Cowboys looked after the cattle on the long drives north.
   b) Indians sometimes helped cowboys by acting as guides.
   c) All cowboys had exciting lives.
   d) Indians did not like cowboys driving cattle over their lands.
   e) The Indians probably hated the cowboys.

2 Look at source 17. Now read sources 14 and 15 again. It seems, from these sources, that Indians were often friendly to cowboys. Source 16 suggests that a cowboy's way of life was very like an Indian's. Why do you think, then, that so many cowboy films have shown cowboys and Indians as implacable enemies?

3 Do you think that cowboys and Indians *were* sworn enemies? Try to explain what you think about this. If they fought – why did they do so?

Homesteaders

Mormons and miners, cattlemen and cowboys – all, as they moved over the plains, disturbed the way of life of the Plains Indians. They all got on quite well with the Indians, though, as you have read, there were one or two nasty incidents. What if people began to move onto the Plains in large numbers? What if they found that the Indians were in their way?

Not many people seriously thought that anyone but the Indians could live on the Plains. They certainly didn't think that anyone could farm the land and grow crops. An observer who made an expedition across the Plains in 1820 had this to say about the area:

It is almost wholly unfit for cultivation, and of course uninhabitable by a people depending upon agriculture for their subsistence [living].

Edwin James, in *Early Western Travels, 1748–1846*

Big Elk, a member of the Ponca Indians, told the story of his life to a white man who wrote it all down. He agreed with Edwin James.

For although I am but a poor simple Indian, yet I know that this land will not suit your farmers; if I ever thought your hearts bad enough to take the land. I would not fear it, as I know there is not wood enough on it for the use of whites.

W. P. Webb, *The Great Plains*, 1824

They were both wrong. By the end of the nineteenth century thousands of families had settled on the Plains and were growing crops successfully. There were many reasons why this happened. Families who wanted to start a new life in the 1840s and 1850s crossed over the Plains to settle in California or Oregon. By the 1860s most of the land there was being farmed and was becoming expensive to buy. For ordinary men and women in search of land and a new start in life, the Great Plains offered them their only chance. Some of these people had been slaves in the southern states until slavery was ended in the 1860s. Others came over from Europe, trying to get away from poverty and unemployment there. Most, however, were Americans from the states east of the Mississippi River.

The US Government wanted people to settle on the Great Plains, so the Government helped people to get land cheaply. It also made sure that there was law and order in the newly settled areas. The one thing which made it all possible, though, was the railroad. People could travel with their belongings on a train much more easily than in a wagon. More than this, the United States Government gave the railroad companies the land near their railroads. They sold this to the settlers and used the money to build more railroads.

How did all this affect the Indians? The settlers themselves were not the problem. It was only when the US Government decided that the Indians were in the way that the trouble started.

20 A railroad advertisement for land, 1875.

1 This railroad company is clearly trying to get people to buy land. Make a list of the different things which the company is offering to people who want to buy land from the Burlington and Missouri River Railroad Co.

21 People moving West on the railroad

2 Look at source 21 which shows people travelling west, and read sources **9** and **10**. Make a list of all the problems which people had when they travelled by wagon. Would travelling by train solve all those problems? Would there be any new problems for train travellers? If so, do you think they were worse than the ones suffered by wagon travellers?

Review and Assessment

1 At the beginning of the nineteenth century, only the Indians lived on the Great Plains. By the end of the century many other people had moved westwards and were living and working on the Plains. Describe, as carefully as you can, the changes which took place on the Great Plains between 1800 and 1900.

2 Not everything on the Great Plains changed. Can you think of any things which remained the same?

3 *People find gold on the Plains.*
Farmers move onto the Plains.
Cattlemen begin to raise cattle on the Plains.
New States are made in the Plains area. These become part of the United States of America.
Railroads cross the Plains and join East and West.
Farmers set up windpumps to draw up water.
Barbed wire keeps cattlemen out of farmers' lands.
The way of life of the Plains Indians is disturbed by people who move onto their lands.

Above is a list of some of the things which happened on the Great Plains during the nineteenth century. Copy this table and try to fit each of them under one of the headings below.

ECONOMIC CHANGE	POLITICAL CHANGE	TECHNOLOGICAL CHANGE	SOCIAL CHANGE

4 Who gained from all these changes? Who lost? Think carefully about this and explain your answer as carefully and in as much detail as you can.

7 The struggle for the Plains

1 'Across the Continent', a drawing by Fanny Palmer. She lived in North America and knew the Plains well. This is not, however, a drawing of a real place.

By the 1880s the Great Plains were no longer thought of as the Great American Desert. As you have seen, early settlers and miners travelled over them. Cattle trails and railroads crossed them. Then the homesteaders settled on the Plains and farmed them. We have not yet seen what the Indians who lived and hunted in these areas felt about these white Americans and the 'iron horse' – the steam train which puffed noisily over their lands.

Way back in 1832 the US Government had said that the whole of the Great Plains would be given over to the Indian tribes. This was so that white people could have all the lands in the eastern states without the Indians getting in the way. They started moving some Indians from these states as early as 1825. By 1840 the government had moved all the Indian tribes who lived in the eastern states, like the Cherokees and the Seminoles, into 'Indian Territory' on the Plains. They joined those who already lived on the Plains, like the Arapahos, the Sioux and the Comanches, behind an imaginary line known as the Permanent Indian Frontier. You can see this on the map (source 4).

Then white people started to cross Indian land! No wonder the Indians often attacked them. The white people who crossed Indian land soon demanded protection from Indian attacks. Francis Parkman described some of the white people he met on the Oregon Trail in the 1840s.

2 *They were ill-looking fellows, thin and swarthy, with care-worn, anxious faces. . . Some of their party had died; one man had been killed by the Pawnees; and about a week before they had been plundered by the Dahcotahs [Sioux] of all their best horses.*

Francis Parkman, *The Oregon Trail*, 1968

1 Look back on the section on the mountain men (Chapter 6, pages 45–46). Read source 6 on page 46. Why, to begin with, were most Indians friendly towards white people, in the mountain areas and on the Plains?

2 Read source 2. This tells a different story. Why did Indian attacks on white people increase? Read these suggestions.
a) Some tribes were more hostile than others.
b) Francis Parkman was lying.
c) The Government encouraged travellers to kill Indians who came near wagon trains and camps.
d) Indians began to feel threatened as more and more white people crossed the Plains.
e) Many travellers, like some miners, did not respect the rights of the Indians as the mountain men had done.
Take each suggestion and explain whether or not you agree with it. Can you think of any other reasons? Does the drawing (source 1) help you to understand how the Indians felt about white settlers and trains?

3 What did the Indians gain from the Fort Laramie Treaty?
4 What did white people gain from the Fort Laramie Treaty?
5 Who do you think gained more – Indians or white people? Explain your answer.

The Plains Indians were much more determined to defend their lands than any of the other Indians who came into contact with white people. This was because the Plains Indians were wandering hunters who needed to be able to freely to follow the herds of buffalo. Other Indians, like the Snake, the Bannock and the Ute tribes who lived in the northern mountains, did not hunt and live off the buffalo.

The US Government made agreements with several Indian tribes between 1849 and 1851. The idea was that each tribe should have its own hunting grounds, away from white people's trails, and away from other tribes. The trails would then be safe. The Indians agreed with this, but only because the treaties gave them lands – 'forever' – along the foothills of the Rockies between the North Platte and Arkansas Rivers. This was all put together in a big treaty which both sides agreed to in 1851, at Fort Laramie.

> **3**
>
> *Article 1:* *The Indian nations to make an effective and lasting peace.*
>
> *Article 2:* *The Indian nations do hereby recognize the right of the United States Government to establish roads, military and other posts, within their territories.*
>
> *Article 3:* *The United States bind themselves to protect the Indian nations against all depredations* [attacks to seize property or land] *by the people of the United States.*
>
> *Article 5:* [This Article described the lands which were to be given to the different Indian nations.]
>
> *Article 7:* *The United States bind themselves to deliver to the Indian nations the sum of fifty thousand dollars per annum for the term of ten years in provisions, merchandise, domestic animals and agricultural implements.*

Extracts from the Treaty made at Fort Laramie on 17 September 1851

So Indians agreed to allow roads and military posts to be built. In return the Government would protect them and give them $50,000 a year for ten years. The tribes were put in different parts of the Plains. The Indians didn't realise just what a clever move this was by the Government. If the tribes were separated it would be much easier to force one group to give up its land to the Government in the future. Separation would prevent other tribes from supporting others whose lands were threatened.

Within a few years it was clear that these treaties were not working. Trouble started again in Colorado, where the Cheyennes and the Arapahos had settled. In 1859 gold was discovered at Pike's Peak in the Colorado Mountains. In the rush for gold, the white men who surged through the Cheyenne and Arapaho lands forgot agreements made with the Indians. In 1861, the US Government declared that Colorado was part of the United States of America.

4 **Lands of the Plains Indians in 1865.**

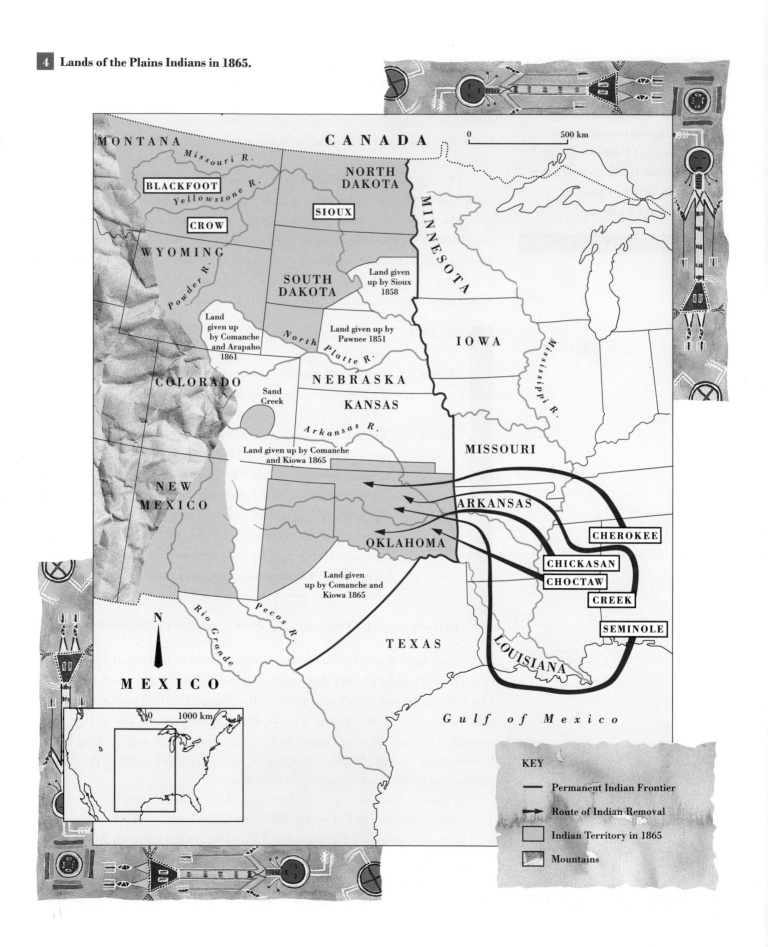

MONTANA

CANADA

0   500 km

Missouri R.

NORTH
DAKOTA

BLACKFOOT

Yellowstone R.

SIOUX

CROW

MINNESOTA

WYOMING

Powder R.

SOUTH
DAKOTA

Land given
up by Sioux
1858

IOWA

Land
given up
by Comanche
and Arapaho
1861

*North
Platte R.*

Land given up by
Pawnee 1851

Mississippi R.

COLORADO

NEBRASKA

KANSAS

Sand
Creek

Arkansas R.

MISSOURI

NEW
MEXICO

Land given up by Comanche
and Kiowa 1865

ARKANSAS

CHEROKEE

OKLAHOMA

CHICKASAN

CHOCTAW

Land given
up by Comanche and
Kiowa 1865

CREEK

N

Rio Grande

Pecos R.

SEMINOLE

TEXAS

LOUISIANA

MEXICO

Gulf of Mexico

0   1000 km

KEY

——— **Permanent Indian Frontier**

——▶ **Route of Indian Removal**

☐ **Indian Territory in 1865**

▦ **Mountains**

1 Look back at the maps on page 47 (source 8) and page 49 (source 11). Now look carefully at the map on page 60. How do the earlier maps help to explain why the area between the North Platte and Arkansas Rivers became a fierce battleground between Indians and white people? Explain your answer in as much detail as you can.

The Indians, however, remembered the white men's promises. They began serious attacks on the railroad surveyors and travellers.

The Government called the chiefs from these tribes to a meeting at Fort Lyon. Government officials forced them to give up the claim to the land which had been given to them earlier. Instead they were given a piece of land between the Arkansas River and Sand Creek in eastern Colorado. White men called this land a 'reservation'. The problem was that Indian chiefs had no power to force their people to do anything. Many warriors refused to accept what the chiefs had agreed. They went on the war-path. They raided mining camps and attacked mail coaches. The agreements made at Fort Lyon did not work at all. For several years there was fierce warfare as the Indians fought to stop white people taking away from them the lands which the US Government had earlier given them 'forever'.

The Plains Wars

In the early hours of 29 November 1864 a regiment of 1000 men, with their leader, Colonel John Chivington, quietly surrounded an Indian camp at Sand Creek, Colorado. At daybreak the soldiers charged the camp. They took the Indians completely by surprise. The story is continued by Robert Bent, a Cheyenne half-breed son of a rancher. Chivington had forced him to go as a guide in the search for the Indian camp:

2 All over the world people accepted the white flag as a sign of surrender. Black Kettle and his people even waved the American flag. Why do you think the soldiers ignored the flags and shot all the Indians? The rest of this section and pages 57–60 will help you to answer the question fully.

> 5 *I saw the American flag waving and heard Black Kettle [a Cheyenne chief] tell the Indians to stand around the flag, and there they were huddled – men, women and children. This was when we were within fifty yards of the Indians. I also saw a white flag raised. These flags were in so conspicuous [obvious] a position that they must have been seen. I think there were six hundred Indians in all. I think there were thirty-five braves and some old men, about sixty in all. The rest of the men were away from camp, hunting. I saw five squaws under a bank for shelter. When the troops came up to them they ran out and begged for mercy, but the soldiers shot them all.*

The US Congress 39th, 2nd Session, Senate Report 156

Why did this happen? For about three years, Indians had been raiding and attacking the army and white people. They were trying to get back the lands which they believed were theirs. The soldiers in the local regiments were determined to fight back. They did not really want to stop the fighting. In

 Chivington and his men charge the Indians at Sand Creek, 1864. A contemporary painting.

August 1864 Black Kettle went to the commander at Fort Lyon to ask for peace. The commander, Major Edward Wynkoop, told Black Kettle that he could not end the fighting. He went to the Governor of Colorado. Governor Evans refused to accept Black Kettle's surrender. 'What shall I do with the 3rd Colorado Regiment if I make peace?' he said. 'They have been raised to kill Indians and they must kill Indians.' Black Kettle returned and set up camp at Sand Creek. Some Arapahos, who were camping close to Fort Lyon, joined the Cheyenne for safety.

It was then that Colonel Chivington and his men attacked. Black Kettle managed to escape, and carried the news of the massacre to other tribes. As a result of this the Cheyennes, the Arapahos, the Comanches and the Kiowas increased their attacks on ranches, travellers and mail coaches throughout the winter of 1864–5. The soldiers hit back fiercely. In the end, both sides – Indians and soldiers – wanted an end to the wars.

Indian chiefs and Government officials finally met, in October 1865, at Bluff Creek. The Cheyennes, Arapahos, Kiowa-Apaches, Kiowas and Comanches agreed to give up their traditional claims to land and to go to reservations. There was peace in the south-western Plains, but it was not the end of the Plains Wars. The Sioux were still resisting the US Government in the northern Plains. They specially resented a new trail – the Powder River Road – which was being blazed over their best hunting country, the foothills of the Big Horn Mountains. Cheyennes and Arapahos joined the Sioux in their fight against this trail.

This is what Red Cloud, a Sioux Chief, said about the trail:

> 7 *Whose voice was first sounded on this land? The voice of my people who had bows and arrows. What has been done in my country I did not want, did not ask for it; white people going through my country. When the white man comes in my country he leaves a trail of blood behind him. I have two mountains in that country – the Black Hills and the Big Horn Mountain. I want the Great Father* [the US President] *to make no roads through them.*

Dee Brown, *Bury My Heart at Wounded Knee*, 1971

8 **Chief Red Cloud of the Oglala Sioux**

Treaties and reservations

In 1867–8 the Government held a series of meetings with all the Indian tribes who were still fighting them. They now believed that the best idea was to put the Indian tribes separately in small reservations. They would learn how to become farmers and to live the way of life of white people. They would be out of the way of settlers, miners and soldiers. The Government thought that two places were ideal for these new small reservations. One was Oklahoma, where the eastern tribes had been moved in the 1830s. The other was the Black Hills of Dakota. No one thought that any white people would want to settle in the Black Hills. They were far too hilly and a long way from the main routes across the US.

The Southern Plains Indians, including the Kiowas, the Cheyenne and the Arapahos, made a treaty with the Government at Medicine Lodge Creek in October 1867. The Northern Plains Indians, including the Sioux and the Navaho, also agreed to a treaty, at Fort Laramie, in April 1868. You can see the places to which they all moved on the map (source 11). The treaty which Red Cloud, the Sioux leader, signed at Fort Laramie seems to show the Indians' and white people's hopes.

> 9 *From this day forward all war between the parties to this agreement shall forever cease. The government of the United States desires peace, and its honor is hereby pledged to keep it. The Indians desire peace, and they now pledge their honor to maintain it.*

Treaty signed at Fort Laramie, April 1868

Would Indians and white people both now be able to live as they wished in peace? Both sides had problems which made this impossible. The Plains Indians could not live their old nomadic way of life in the reservations. Many of them were miserable, unable to settle to farming, and longed to return to the

1 **Look back to Chapter 5 and read again what it says about cattlemen, railroads and homesteaders on the Plains.**
a) What sort of argument do you think Red Cloud would have used to fight the building of the Powder River Road? Use source 7 and this chapter to help you.
b) What arguments do you think the US Government would have used to answer him?

open plains to hunt buffalo. It was difficult for Indians to accept the idea that land could be sold. As Crazy Horse said, 'One does not sell the earth upon which the people walk.'

What did white people feel about all this? Here is a soldier's view:

10 *We have now selected and provided reservations for all. All who cling to their old hunting grounds are hostile and will remain so till killed off.*

Army commander, Western Plains, September 1868

1 Sources 9 and 10 were both written by white Americans.
a) Choose words from this list to describe the tone of each source: *hopeful, arrogant, equal, hostile, friendly, honest.*
b) Which of the two sources do you think better shows what white Americans felt about the Plains Indians?

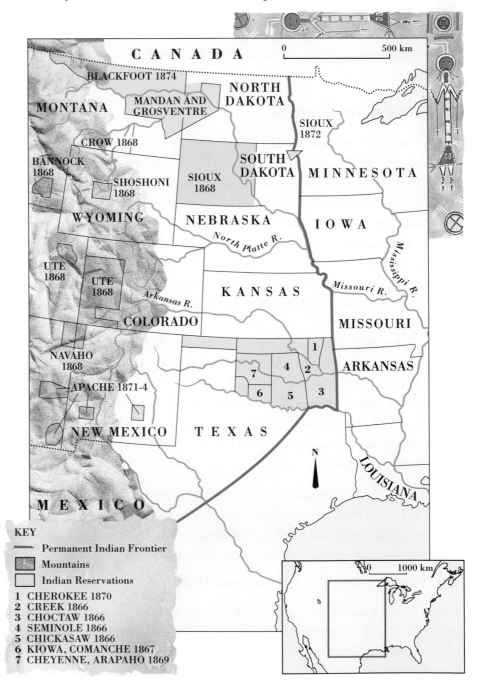

11 Indian reservations in 1875.

KEY
— Permanent Indian Frontier
Mountains
Indian Reservations
1 CHEROKEE 1870
2 CREEK 1866
3 CHOCTAW 1866
4 SEMINOLE 1866
5 CHICKASAW 1866
6 KIOWA, COMANCHE 1867
7 CHEYENNE, ARAPAHO 1869

The Army takes control

It was not long before trouble began again. Some Indian warriors could not accept the treaties which their chiefs made with the white people. They went on the war-path, attacking white people and their homes.

The reservations were not working, either. The idea behind these was that Indians should learn the white people's way of life. They would learn how to use a plough and reap a crop of corn. They would go to school and learn how to read, write and do simple sums. The US Government did not realise that learning the white people's way of life was the most difficult thing in the world for Indians to do.

12 *The whites were always trying to make the Indians give up their life and live like white men, and the Indians did not know how to do that, and did not want to anyway.*

Big Eagle, a Sioux chieftain, 1862

If the Indians were to live like white people they would have to learn to think about the land in a totally different way. This was more than many of them could do. Indians believed that land could not be bought and sold. It was there for people to use but also to look after. They never tried to change the land around them. Instead they worked with the land and tried to understand the powerful forces which they felt lay within it.

White people had quite different ideas about the land. Their God had told them to 'Be fruitful and multiply, and replenish the earth and subdue it' (Genesis, Chapter 1, verse 28). What clearer command did man need to plough the earth and sow and reap crops?

Sherman shows the way

Some army officers wanted the Plains Indians to be killed off once and for all.

13 *The more we can kill this year, the less will have to be killed next year.*

Major-General William T. Sherman, 1868

The commander of the army in the West, General Philip H. Sheridan, decided to plan a winter campaign. This was a clever move. It would be easier to attack the Indians in their winter camps than to track down all the roving bands in the summer. Troops would drive the Indians into the Washita River Valley in Indian Territory. Here General Custer and his troops would crush the Indians. Before this, however, Custer and his men came across a fresh Indian trail, he dashed after the Indians until he reached their camp on 26 November 1868. Chief Black Kettle and several hundred Cheyenne and Arapaho warriors had camped for the night. At dawn the troops rushed the camp and took the Indians by surprise. After a short time the Indians were completely defeated.

Custer's attack finally broke the spirits of the Indians in that area. In January 1869 Custer took the remaining Indian chiefs to Fort Cobb, on the Washita River. They signed treaties agreeing to go to reservations.

Dee Brown, who spent many years finding out about the American Indians, wrote about the events after the mustering of the Indians at Fort Cobb:

14 *Yellow Bear of the Arapahos also agreed to bring his people to Fort Cobb. A few days later, Tosawi brought in the first band of Comanches to surrender. When he was presented to Sheridan, Tosawi's eyes brightened. He spoke his own name and added two words of broken English. 'Tosawi, good Indian,' he said. It was then that General Sheridan uttered the immortal words 'The only good Indians I ever saw were dead.'*

Dee Brown, *Bury My Heart at Wounded Knee*, 1971

Meanwhile, Indian attacks continued in Texas. Major-General Sherman replaced General Sheridan as commander of the army on the Plains. He noticed everywhere signs of Indian attacks and raids. He was in no mood to be kind to Indians. They must be punished! Sherman sent his troops against the Indians in the Red River area. There was fierce fighting throughout the winter of 1874–5. By summer 1875 the Indians could resist no longer. War-weary, half-starved and broken, they went back to their reservations in Indian Territory.

The pictures and the written sources on these pages show the different views of Indians and white people. Look back at Chapter 4 and look again at what you have read so far in Chapter 7.

1 What do you think were the main differences between Indians and white people?

2 Look at sources 1, 6, 15 and 16. How do these help to show us the different ways in which white people felt about Indians?

3 Why were white people, in the end, able to force Indians to go into reservations?

15 'Attack at Dawn'. This painting by Charles Schreyvogel shows Custer and his men attacking Black Kettle in his Washita River Valley camp. Schreyvogel did not go to the American West until the 1890s, though he did spend some time on an Indian reservation in Ute, Colorado.

16 A white American made this painting of Indians attacking homesteaders during the late nineteenth century.

The Battle of the Little Big Horn

In the early 1870s there was trouble with the Sioux in their Dakota reservation in the Black Hills. They complained that their food was bad and that they had too few blankets. They were worried because trains on the Northern Pacific Railroad steamed across their hunting grounds. These brought hordes of hunters who killed buffalo for their skins to sell in the East. This was another way in which white people and Indians differed.

17 *Has the white man become a child that he should recklessly kill and not eat? When the red men slay game, they do so that they may live and not starve.*

Chief Santana of the Kiowa, in Dee Brown, *Bury My Heart at Wounded Knee*, 1971

In 1874 General Custer was sent to the Black Hills to find out whether a fort could be built there to protect the railroad. Then Custer's army discovered gold in the Black Hills. The Government tried to persuade the Sioux to sell the Black Hills area. Red Cloud demanded $600,000,000. Other Sioux chiefs refused to bargain. The Government did not get the land, but still decided to send in prospectors for gold. Thousands poured in during the winter of 1875. They claimed the land which the Sioux believed was theirs.

Trouble soon began. Some Sioux braves slipped away from their reservations. The Government ordered them back. Sitting Bull and Crazy Horse of the Teton Sioux refused to return and prepared for war. The Government ordered the army to force them back to their reservation.

The Indians gather at the Rosebud River

During the spring of 1876 thousands of Sioux Indians gathered along the banks of the Rosebud River (see the map on page 69). Bands of Cheyenne and Arapaho Indians joined them. They all remembered well the times when white people had threatened their people before.

The Sioux Chief, Sitting Bull, had a vision during the sun dance which his tribe held in June 1876. He told the rest of the Indians that he had seen soldiers falling head first into their camp. The Indians believed that this meant that they would defeat the soldiers. They would then be able to remove the white people from their sacred hunting grounds in the Black Hills.

The Army's plan

Here, at last, seemed to be a chance to wipe out thousands of hostile Indians! General Sheridan ordered Brigadier-General George Crook, Brigadier-General

18 Chief Sitting Bull

19 General George Armstrong Custer

20 The area around the Little Big Horn.

Alfred H. Terry and Colonel John Gibbon to move in on the Indians at the Rosebud River. General George A. Custer went with Terry as commander of the 7th US Cavalry.

The first disaster was on 17 June 1876. General Crook and his men met Chief Crazy Horse with 1000 braves near the source of the Rosebud River. General Crook was forced to withdraw. The Indians returned to their camp in triumph.

The Indian chiefs then decided to move camp west to the valley of the Little Big Horn River. They set up camp with more than 10,000 squaws, braves and children.

After General Terry's and Colonel Gibbon's men met, Terry's scouts found an Indian trail leading westwards towards the Little Big Horn River. Terry sent Colonel Gibbon and his infantry to the mouth of the Little Big Horn River to attack from the north. The much faster 7th Cavalry was sent to attack from the south. Terry knew that the cavalry would make a much fiercer attack than the infantry. He offered Custer the help of the 2nd US Cavalry which had been with Gibbons' force. Custer refused help. Terry knew that Custer had disobeyed orders before. He gave Custer his orders in writing and told him that he must obey them.

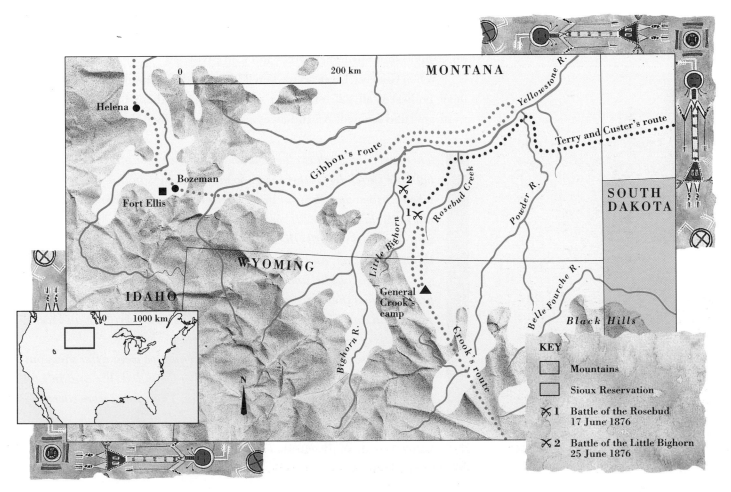

Custer's last stand

Custer and the US 7th Cavalry set off up the Rosebud River on 24 June 1876. In the evening, after a journey of 46 kilometres, Custer halted his men. Later that evening he heard from his scouts that the Sioux had left the Rosebud River and were approaching the Little Big Horn River. Custer made up his mind. He would attack without the support of Gibbons. He could not take the Indian camp by surprise. He would attack at once. He split his men into three divisions. Captain Benteen was sent with 125 men to the south. Major Reno was to advance along the south bank of a stream which ran into the Little Big Horn River. Custer himself would go along the north bank of the stream.

Reno was beaten back after a fierce fight on the banks of the Little Big Horn River. Those who were left met Benteen and his men who had found no Indians. Reno and his men were just setting off to go to Custer's aid when hundreds of Indians appeared and drove them back onto the hilltop. A fierce ring of Indian warriors kept them there until darkness fell.

Meanwhile, Custer was fighting for his life. Chief Gall of the Sioux, who had beaten back Major Reno, charged up from the south. Crazy Horse, who had defeated General Crook, swept right round Custer's position from the north. Other bands surged in until Custer and his men were surrounded. Archaeologists who have recently dug in the site of the battle have proved that the Indians were armed with the latest repeating rifles. The US soldiers used only single-shot Springfield rifles and Colt revolvers.

When General Terry arrived on 27 June with the main army he found the dead bodies of all 225 of Custer's men. Most of them had been stripped, mutilated and scalped. An Indian eye-witness described the battle.

21 *There was not much excitement and at first we thought it would be better to surrender as there were so many soldiers in this country, but when Custer came in sight there were not so many. We sneaked from our tents through the tall grass to where our ponies were picketed [tied up]. We raced towards the soldiers as the bullets came switching through the grass and through the leaves of the trees.*

And we fought, and the soldiers fought, and when we chased the first lot across the river we turned and went for those on the hills. The smoke and dust were very thick — you couldn't see anything and we killed lots of our own men because they got in the way.

Pretty soon the soldiers began to run and we went after them but it wasn't long before they were all killed or wounded. We couldn't tell who was Custer, we couldn't tell anything. Their faces were covered with dust and their eyes and mouths were full of it.'

Quoted by B. W. Beacroft, *The Last Fighting Indians in the American West*, 1976

Much later, Dee Brown wrote a book in which he put together many of the things which Indians said about the battle.

22 *Long after the battle, White Bull of the Minneconjous drew four pictographs showing himself grappling with and killing a soldier identified as Custer. Among others who claimed to have killed Custer were Rain-in-the-Face, Flat Hip and Brave Bear. Red Horse said that an unidentified Santee warrior killed Custer. Most Indians who told of the battle said they never saw Custer and did not know who killed him.*

In an interview given in Canada a year after the battle Sitting Bull said that he never saw Custer, but that other Indians had seen and recognized him just before he was killed. 'He did not wear his long hair as he used to wear it'. Sitting Bull said. 'It was short, but it was the colour of the grass when the frost comes.' But Sitting Bull did not say who killed Custer.

Dee Brown, *Bury My Heart at Wounded Knee*, 1971

23 A reconstruction of the Battle of the Little Big Horn, painted by Edgar Paxson in 1899 after a good deal of research. You can see Custer in the top centre of the picture.

24 Kicking Bear, an Indian, painted this picture of the Battle of the Little Big Horn. This is the only eye-witness drawing which is known to exist. Custer is lying to the left of centre. Standing in the centre (left to right) are Sitting Bull, Rain-in-the-Face, Crazy Horse and Kicking Bear.

1 We know very little about what happened at the Battle of the Little Big Horn. No white man survived. The Indians who survived wouldn't say very much. Look at sources 23 and 24.

a) What differences can you see in the way in which these two artists draw the battle?

b) What reasons can you suggest to explain these differences?

c) Which of the two do you think is likely to be the more accurate? Why?

d) Do sources 21 and 22 back up the paintings of the battle (sources 23 and 24)?

2 Find the evidence in source 21 which shows

a) that the Indians were expecting to find more US soldiers than they did;

b) that it was difficult to see what was happening in the battle.

3 Why do you think so many Indians (source 22) claimed to have killed Custer?

4 Why did the Indians defeat Custer and the 7th US Cavalry? Use the sources in this section as well as what you have read to help you to answer this.

Review and Assessment

1 In this chapter you have read about all the different people who were involved in the 'struggle for the Plains'. Use what you have read, including the sources and also the pictures, to help you to suggest
  a How Francis Parkman felt towards the Plains Indians;
  b What Red Cloud might have felt after the Fort Laramie Treaty in 1868;
  c What Major-General William T. Sherman thought of the Plains Indians;
  d What Kicking Bear (who drew the picture in source 24) might have felt about the Battle of the Little Big Horn.

2 Not all the white men listed above felt the same about the Indians (for example, Francis Parkman and General Sherman). Why was this so? The Indians in the list felt differently at different times. Why?

3 'All white people hated the Indians. All Indians were hostile towards white people.' We cannot say this. Why not? Explain your answer as fully as you can.

8 The end of the Indian way of life

Was the Battle of the Little Big Horn really a victory for the Indians?

The news of the terrible defeat of General Custer and the 7th US Cavalry spread quickly. People were stunned and horrified. They began to talk about crushing the Plains Indians once and for all. After the battle, the Sioux and the Cheyenne bands separated and went away. The US army chased them fiercely until they caught them. By the autumn of 1876 most of these Indians were back in their reservations. Crazy Horse fought against the army but was captured in September 1877. He tried to escape but was killed.

Was this the end of the Plains Indians? Not quite, as we shall see. Sitting Bull had not completely given up hope. He would do all he could to keep the lands which the Sioux believed were theirs. In October 1890, Kicking Bear, a Minneconjou Indian, came to Sitting Bull with a strange story. He told him that a Paiute medicine man, Wovoka, had had a vision. The vision told him to say this to the Indians:

All Indians must dance, everywhere, keep on dancing. Pretty soon in the next Spring Great Spirit come. He bring back game of every kind. All dead Indians come back and live again. When Great Spirit comes this way, then all Indians go to mountains, high up away from whites. Whites can't hurt Indians then. Then while Indians way up high, big

flood comes like water and all white people die. After that, water go away and then nobody but Indians everywhere and game all kinds thick.

Wovoka, in Dee Brown, *Bury my Heart at Wounded Knee*, 1971

Kicking Bear told Sitting Bull that if the Indians wore special shirts, painted with magic symbols, the soldiers' bullets would not harm them when they danced the Dance of the Ghosts. Soon Indians everywhere were dancing the Dance of the Ghosts. Perhaps they could bring back their dead brothers and sisters. Perhaps, soon, the Plains would be covered with herds of buffalo. Perhaps white people would soon be gone from Indian lands. Wovoka told the Indians, 'You must not hurt anybody. You must not fight.' Even so, some of the dancers held rifles over their heads as they danced. White people became very worried.

2 The Ghost Dancers' Song

Father, have pity on us
We are crying for thirst
All is gone!
We have nothing to eat
Father, we are poor.
We are very poor.
The buffalo are all gone.
They are all gone.
Take pity on us, Father.
We are dancing as you wished
Because you commanded us.
Help us to be what we once
*   were*
Happy hunters of buffalo.

3 Arapaho Indians doing the ghost dance, 1893.

4 Wovoka with Arapaho chiefs.

1 The Indians believed that the ghost dance would bring back their old way of life. White people did not believe this. How would an Arapaho Indian explain what she or he felt about the ghost dance? How would a white US soldier explain what he felt about the Indians doing a ghost dance?

The Battle of Wounded Knee

Early on 15 December 1890, 43 members of the police who guarded the Indian reservations surrounded Sitting Bull's log cabin. They had come to arrest Sitting Bull because he was encouraging the ghost dance. Crowds of ghost dancers soon gathered round. In the confusion which followed, Sitting Bull was shot and killed, together with several other Indians and half a dozen policemen.

The Sioux did not give up hope of getting back to their old way of life. Big Foot, another Sioux chief, took his people down to Red Cloud's Pine Ridge reservation. Big Foot was ill, and travelling in a wagon. On their way they met part of the US 7th Cavalry. The Indians surrendered. The soldiers took the 350 men, women and children to a military post at Wounded Knee Creek. There they camped. The soldiers guarded them closely in case anyone tried to escape.

Next morning the soldiers ordered the Indians to give up their guns and any other weapons. One young warrior refused to give up his rifle and there was a struggle. A shot was heard and the soldiers began to shoot. The Indians fought with what weapons they still had and grappled hand to hand. The soldiers then turned their guns on the women and the children. Soon Big Foot and most of his people were dead or badly wounded.

A blizzard prevented the army from removing the bodies of the Indians. When the snow stopped, they found that the bodies had frozen into strange

5 Chief Big Foot, frozen in the snow, after the Battle of Wounded Knee.

6 One of the special shirts worn by the ghost dancers.

shapes. The soldiers buried the Indians in a trench. They ripped their ghost dance shirts from them as souvenirs. Their special shirts had not turned aside the bullets. The last hopes and the last resistance of the Indians died with Big Foot and his Sioux, in the snow at Wounded Knee.

The end of the Indian way of life

We have followed the story of the Sioux through to its tragic ending. What had happened to the other Indian tribes? Chief Joseph and the Nez Perce from the north-western mountains resisted for a while, but in the end had to go to Indian Territory. Dull Knife, Little Wolf and the Northern Cheyenne also lost heart. They were sent to Red Cloud's Pine Ridge reservation. Geronimo led the Apaches in a fight against the Government from 1881–6. They too, in the end, surrendered. Chief Joseph probably spoke for all the Indians when he said:

I am tired of fighting. Our chiefs are killed. The old men are dead. I am tired. My heart is sick and sad. From where the sun now stands I will fight no more forever.

Chief Joseph, in Dee Brown, *Bury My Heart at Wounded Knee*, 1971

The Indians were now all in reservations. Their lands could be opened up fully for homesteaders, railway builders and miners. The Indians could only survive if they learned the white people's way of life. Had the Sioux, brave hunters and conquerors of the 7th Cavalry, settled down in their reservation on the northern Plains? Would the Cheyenne and the Arapaho, who fought with the Sioux in the Plains Wars in the early 1860s, be content to stay in Indian Territory? Mountain Indians like the Ute, the Bannock and the Shoshone may have found it easier. They were not nomadic and had never depended on hunting for their food. The Plains Indians, though, with the buffalo gone, could do nothing but accept food sent by the US Government. Many were miserable. Many fell ill and died. Geronimo, too, spoke for all Indians, not just his Apaches on their reservation in Indian Territory, when he said:

Our people are decreasing in numbers here, and will continue to decrease unless they are allowed to return to their native land. There is no climate or soil which is equal to that of Arizona. I want to spend my last days there, and be buried among those mountains. If this could be I might die in peace.

S. M. Barrett, *Geronimo, His Own Story*, 1974

9 **Apache Chief Geronimo in a motor car, 1905.**

Yet Geronimo, as you can see in the photograph, lived on. He even had this photograph taken of him in white men's clothing, in a car!

In the end, even Indian Territory was not safe for the Indians. White Americans were so eager to get land that in 1889 President Harrison decided to open up Indian Territory to white people. In 1907, Indian Territory became Oklahoma, one of the United States of America.

Had the Government solved the 'Indian problem'? Let a white man have the last words:

> **10** *The red man was the true American. They have almost gone, but will never be forgotten. The history of how they fought for their country is written in blood, a stain that time cannot grind out. Their God was the sun, their church all out of doors. Their only book was nature and they knew all the pages.*

Charles Russell, *Trails Plowed Under*, 1937

11 This painting was by Wohaw, a Kiowa. He shows himself turning from the buffalo to the cow. He rests his foot on ploughed land, as if accepting a new way of life.

12 A photograph taken in the early twentieth century. The photographer called it 'Sunset of a Dying Race'.

Review and Assessment

1

13 *People were stripping dead soldiers and putting the clothes on themselves. There was a soldier on the ground and he was still kicking. A Dakota rode up to me and said: 'Boy, get off and scalp him.'*

I got off and started to do it. He had short hair and my knife was not very sharp. He ground his teeth and then I shot him in the forehead and got his scalp.

J. Neihardt, *Black Elk Speaks*, 1974

14 *I have seen in days gone by sights horrible and gory, but never did I feel the sickening sensation, the giddy, fainting feeling that came over me when I saw our dead, dying and wounded after this Indian fight. The bugler was stripped naked, and five arrows driven through him while his skull was literally smashed to atoms. Another soldier was shot with four bullets and three arrows, his scalp torn off and his brains knocked out.*

W. A. Bell, *New Tracks in North America*, Vol. 1, 1869

Read the two sources above, and look back at source 16 on page 67. Using *only* these sources, how would you describe the Indians?

2 Now read source 10 and look at source 12. Using *only* these sources, how would you describe the Indians?

3 Did you come to different conclusions in your answers to Questions 1 and 2? Why do you think this was?

4 Look again at the sources which you used for your answers to Questions 1 and 2. Look also at sources 4, 7 and 8. Write a paragraph which explains how the Indians were lazy, good-for-nothing and in the way of what white people wanted to do.
Write a paragraph which explains how the Indians had their own, way of life which was as important to them as white people's ambitions were to them.
Which of these paragraphs do you agree with? Why? Are you biased for or against Indians or white Americans?
Does one or the other of the paragraphs which you have written give a *really* accurate idea of the Plains Indians? Explain your answer carefully.

5 It is very difficult to write about the past in a completely unbiased way. Why do you think this is?

Epilogue

1 The first Indian member of the U.S. Senate, Ben 'Nighthorse' Campbell.

A dying race? Not at all. In 1800 there were over a million Indians in North America. By 1900 there were only about 300,000. Now numbers have risen again to almost a million. It took a long time, but the US Government finally realised that the Indians were there to stay. In 1924 the Government decided to allow the Indians – the first Americans – to become citizens of the United States of America. In 1935 the Government said that the Indians could govern themselves in their reservations. It wasn't until the 1960s that the Indians themselves began to bring back their old customs and to learn to be proud of their past. Now the Sioux are again doing the sun dance. Government doctors are working with Navaho medicine men to cure their people when they are ill. Indians are running successful businesses, even being elected to serve in the Senate.

It is not likely that Indians will ever again roam the Plains on horseback, following the buffalo and living with nature. Too much has happened, too many towns and roads have been built on the Great Plains. Indians want to be proud of their past, but they are looking to the future.

2 *As we approach the twenty-first century I can't help but feel hopeful about our future. Despite everything that's happened to our people throughout history we've managed to hang on to our culture, we've managed to hang on to our sense of being Cherokee. . .*

When people ask where I want the Cherokee nation to be in the twenty-first century I always tell them I want to enter the twenty-first century not on anybody else's terms but on our own terms. Two hundred years from now people will gather right here in this very place and there will be a very strong Cherokee Nation.'

Chief Mankiller's State of the Nation Address to the Cherokee Nation on 1 September 1990